Arthur Hopewell-Smith

Dental Microscopy

Arthur Hopewell-Smith

Dental Microscopy

ISBN/EAN: 9783744693257

Printed in Europe, USA, Canada, Australia, Japan

Cover: Foto ©Andreas Hilbeck / pixelio.de

More available books at **www.hansebooks.com**

DENTAL MICROSCOPY,

BY

A. HOPEWELL SMITH, L.R.C.P., LOND., M.R.C.S., ENG.,

L.D.S. ENG.

LATE ASSISTANT DEMONSTRATOR OF HISTOLOGY AT CHARING CROSS
HOSPITAL MEDICAL SCHOOL.

With Eight Lithograph Plates from the Author's original drawings.

PHILADELPHIA, U.S.A.:
THE S. S. WHITE DENTAL MANUFACTURING COMPANY,
CHESTNUT STREET.

LONDON, ENGLAND:
THE DENTAL MANUFACTURING COMPANY, LIMITED,
6 TO 10, LEXINGTON STREET.

1895.

[*All rights reserved.*]

In Appreciation

of

CHARLES S. TOMES, Esq., M.A., F.R.S.,

the Author

dedicates this work to him.

PREFACE.

THIS hand-book has been written with a two-fold purpose. It is offered to the student of Dental Histology and others interested in this particular branch of Science, with a view of presenting in a concise manner the chief methods of making microscopical preparations; and of enabling the student, through the medium of the illustrations, to recognise the most important features of the dental tissues. To the advanced worker the notes may appear somewhat amplified; but to those who are desirous of acquiring the art of Dental Microscopy, it is hoped that they will prove to be a guide, not exhaustive, but of some value, stimulating original research, and facilitating the means by which this end may be attained.

The author's best thanks are due to Mr. W. H. Dolamore for his revision of the proof-sheets, and for his superintendence of the work during its passage through the press; and also to those gentlemen who have kindly supplied him with their special methods of procedure.

January, 1895.

CONTENTS.

Chapter.	Page.
I.—INTRODUCTORY	1
II.—ON THE PREPARATION OF THE HARD TISSUES	14
III.—ON THE PREPARATION OF THE SOFT TISSUES	26
IV.—ON THE PREPARATION OF THE HARD AND SOFT TISSUES COMBINED	39
V.—ON IMBEDDING AND CUTTING SECTIONS	52
VI.—ON STAINING AND MOUNTING SECTIONS	64
VII.—ON THE INJECTION OF CAPILLARIES, AND ON THE MEASUREMENT AND DELINEATION OF OBJECTS	86
VIII.—ON PHOTO-MICROGRAPHY	94
APPENDIX	108

LIST OF PLATES.

Plate.
I.—Enamel, Striae of Retzius and Nasmyth's Membrane ... *Frontispiece.*

II.—Dentine, Sheaths of Neumann and Interglobular Spaces ... ... *Facing p.* XV.

III.—Development of Teeth in Mammalia ,, XVII.

IV.—Pulp, Peridental Membrane, and Gum, *in situ* ... ... ,, XIX.

V.—Odontoblasts and their Connections ,, XXI.

VI.—Dentine, Absorbent Organ, Cementum, and Alveolar Bone ... ,, XXIII.

VII.—Pulp and Vascular Supply of Soft Tissues ... ... ,, XXV.

VIII.—Varieties of Dentine... ... ,, XXVII.

Description of Plate I.

Fig. 1.—Longitudinal section of enamel, human: ground down: unstained: $\frac{1}{8}$ in. obj. and A ocular: shews (*a*) prisms: (*b*) fissures produced by grinding.

Fig. 2.—Human enamel, decalcified: stained picro-carmine: $\frac{1}{12}$ in. oil immersion and C ocular: shews (*a*) longitudinal section, striæ, and interprismatic substance: (*b*) transverse section of same, shews the outline of the prisms.

Fig. 3.—Striæ of Retzius (human), ground down: stained orange rubine: 1 in. obj. and A ocular: shews (*a*) enamel: (*b*) free edge of enamel: (*c*) striæ of Retzius: (*d*) dentine.

Fig. 4.—Pit in enamel, with Nasmyth's membrane *in situ*: ground down: unstained: $\frac{1}{12}$ in. obj., C ocular: shews (*a*) enamel: (*b*) **Nasmyth's** membrane (*c*) lacunæ: (*d*) interprismatic substance.

Fig. 5.—Lacunal cells from Nasmyth's membrane; decalcified: unstained: $\frac{1}{8}$ in. obj. C ocular: shews (*a*) cells: (*b*) homogeneous matrix.

PLATE II.

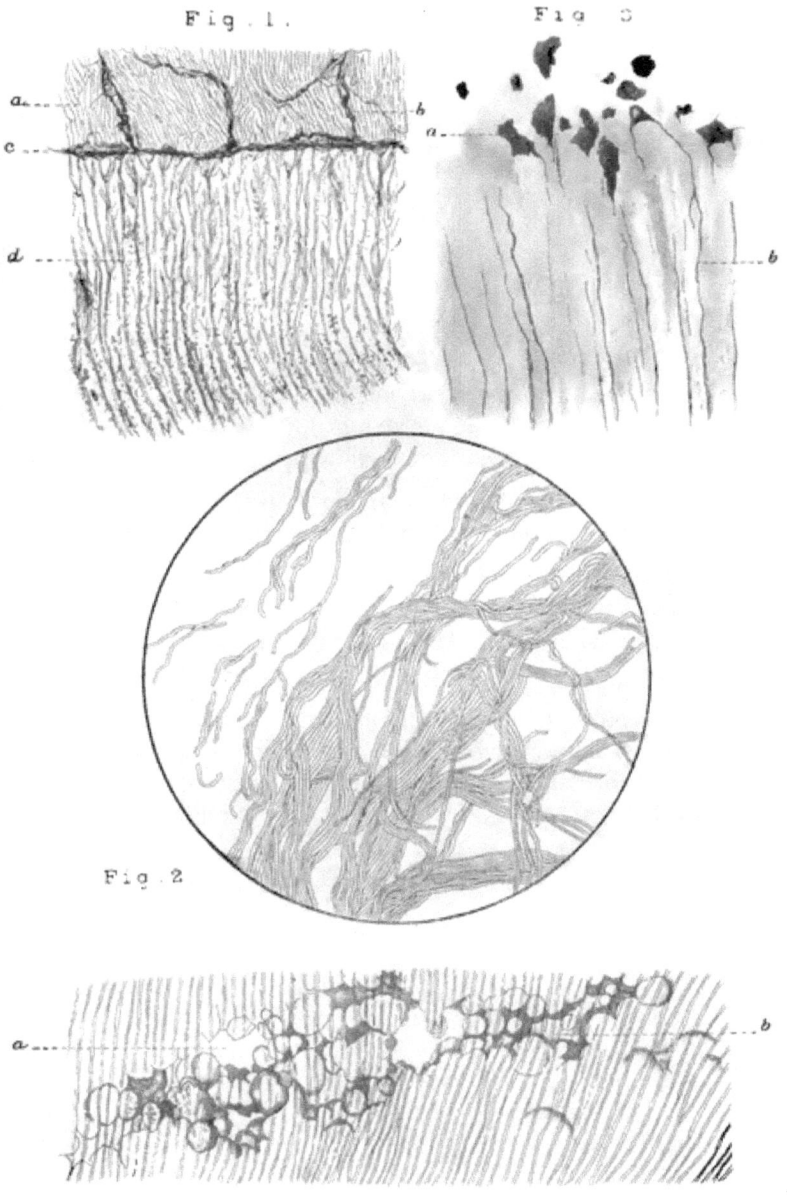

Description of Plate II.

Fig. 1.—Amelo-dentinal junction, longitudinal section: ground down: unstained: ⅙ inch objective and A ocular: shews (*a*) enamel: (*b*) fissures in enamel: (*c*) amelo-dentinal junction: (*d*) dentinal tubules, their branches and terminations.

Fig. 2.—Sheaths of Neumann, decalcified and teased out: carmine: ⅙ inch and A ocular.

Fig. 3.—Dentine, transverse section: ground down: stained methylene blue: ⅙ inch and A ocular: shews (*a*) lacunæ of cementum: (*b*) tubules terminating here and there in lacunæ.

Fig. 4.—Dentine, interglobular spaces, longitudinal section: ground down: unstained: ⅙ inch and A ocular: shews (*a*) interglobular spaces: (*b*) dentinal tubules crossing over the interglobular spaces.

PLATE III

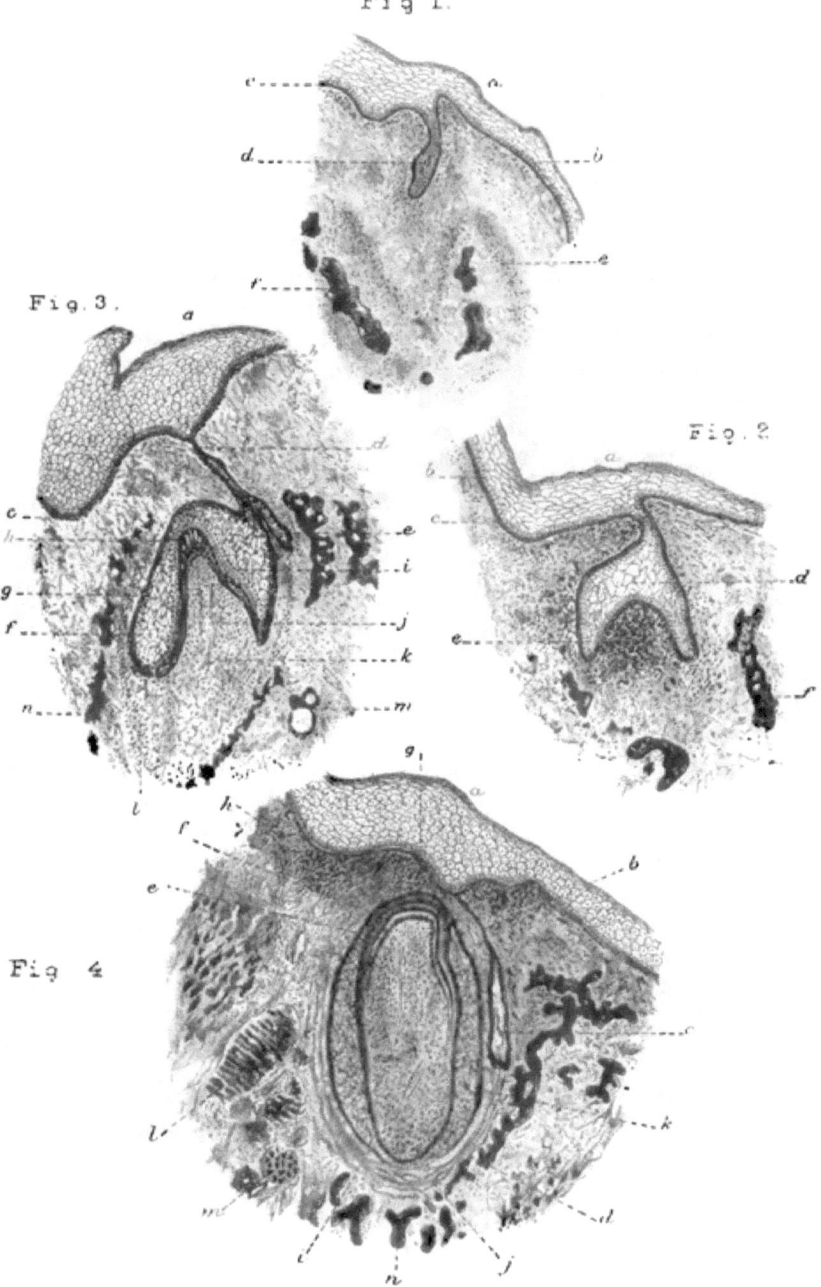

Description of Plate III.

Fig. 1.—This and the accompanying figures are intended to show some of the stages of development of teeth in mammalia. From the embryos of pigs of varying lengths.

First Stage.—Longitudinal section: hardened in perchloride of mercury, or Müller's fluid and alcohol: cut on a microtome: stained hæmatoxylene: 1 inch objective and C ocular: shews (*a*) oral epithelium: (*b*) deeper layer of epithelium: (*c*) Rete Malpighi: (*d*) primary inflection of enamel germ: (*e*) commencement of formation of dental sac: (*f*) bone of jaw.

Fig. 2—*Second Stage.*—Prepared and cut as above: stained carmine: 1 inch and C ocular: shews (*a*) oral epithelium: (*b*) deeper layer of epithelium: (*c*) Rete Malpighi: (*d*) stellate reticulum of enamel organ: (*e*) dentine papilla: (*f*) bone of jaw.

Fig. 3—*Third Stage.*—Prepared and cut as above: stained hæmatoxylene: 1 inch and C ocular: shews (*a*) oral epithelium: (*b*) deep layer of epithelium: (*c*) Rete Malpighi: (*d*) neck of enamel organ: (*e*) permanent enamel germ: (*f*) stellate reticulum of enamel organ: (*g*) external epithelium: (*h*) internal epithelium: (*i*) cells of stratum intermedium: (*j*) dentine papilla: (*k*) rudimentary blood supply of pulp: (*l*) formation of dental sac: (*m*) artery, vein and nerve of jaw: (*n*) bone of jaw.

Fig. 4—*Fourth Stage.*—Prepared and cut as above: stained hæmatoxylene: 2 inch and A ocular: shews (*a*) oral epithelium: (*b*) neck of enamel organ: (*c*) permanent enamel germ: (*d*) dental pulp: (*e*) layer of odontoblasts: (*f*) dentine: (*g*) enamel: (*h*) ameloblasts: (*i*) dental sac, inner portion: (*j*) dental sac, outer portion: (*k*) stellate reticulum: (*l*) muscle fasciculi: (*m*) artery, vein and nerve: (*n*) bone of jaw.

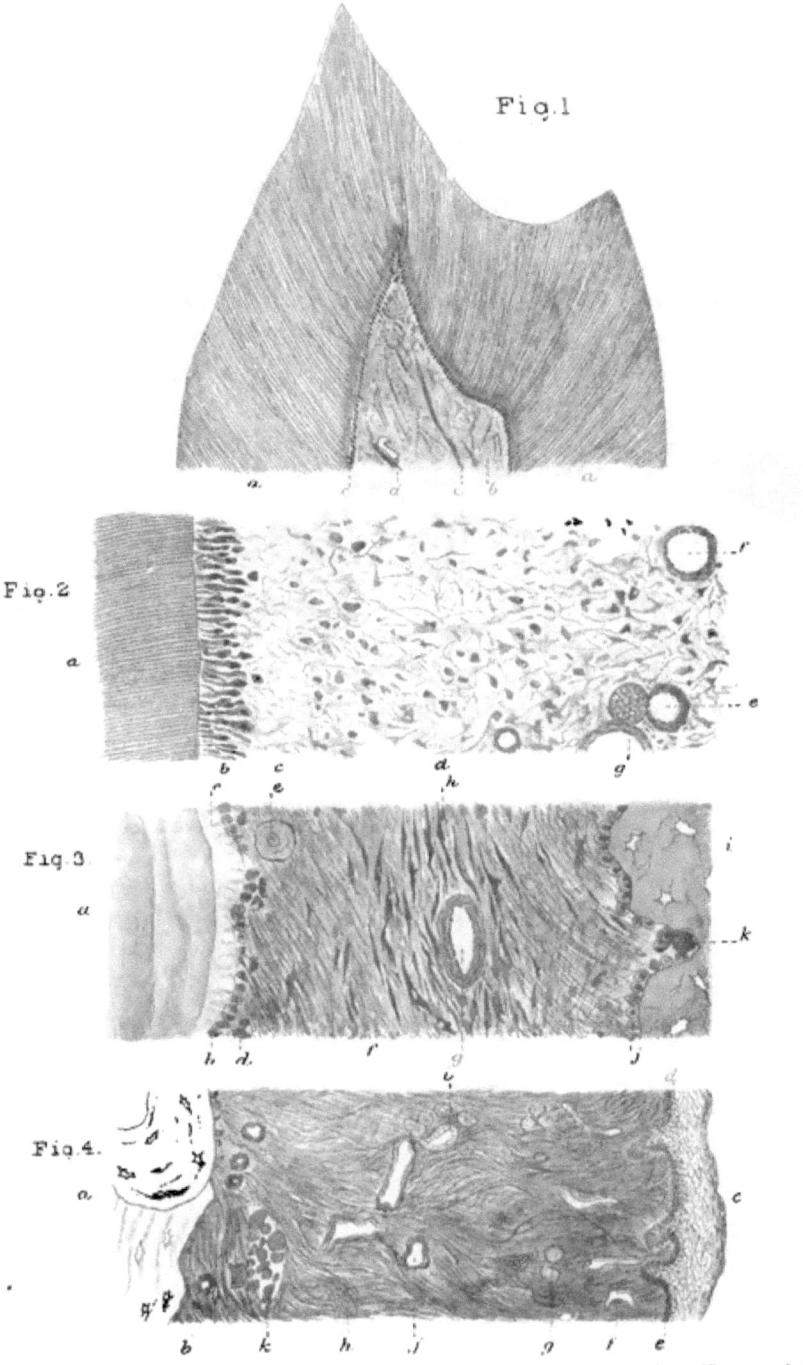

A. Hopewell Smith del.   West, Newman lith

Description of Plate IV.

Fig. 1.—Longitudinal section of crown of bicuspid to show the pulp *in situ:* decalcified (Author's process): stained gold chloride: 2 inch objective and A ocular: shows (a) dentine: (b) pulp *in situ:* (c) membrana eboris: (d) capillary: (e) nerve bundles.

Fig. 2.—Transverse section of pulp *in situ:* young canine tooth below cervical region: decalcified: stained rubine: $\frac{1}{4}$ inch and A ocular: shews (a) dentine: (b) odontoblasts (diagrammatic): (c) basal layer of Weil: (d) pulp tissue: (e) arteriole: (f) venule: (g) nerve bundle.

Fig. 3.—Longitudinal section of peridental membrane *in situ:* decalcified: stained hæmatoxylene: $\frac{1}{4}$ inch and A ocular: shews (a) cementum with lamellæ: (b) cementoblasts: (c) Sharpey's fibres: (d) lymphatics: (e) calcospherite spherule: (f) connective tissue fibres: (g) blood vessel cut obliquely: (h) "principal" fibres of membrane (i) bone of alveolus of jaw: (j) osteoblasts: (k) two osteoclasts.

Fig. 4.—Transverse section of gum *in situ:* decalcified: stained rubine: 2 inch and C ocular: shews (a) bone of alveolus: (b) its periosteum: (c) oral epithelium (stratified): (d) deeper layer of epithelium: (e) Rete Malpighi: (f) submucous tissue: (g) "glands" of Serres: (h) fasciculi of fibrous tissue: (i) mucous glands: (j) blood vessels: (k) muscle fibres.

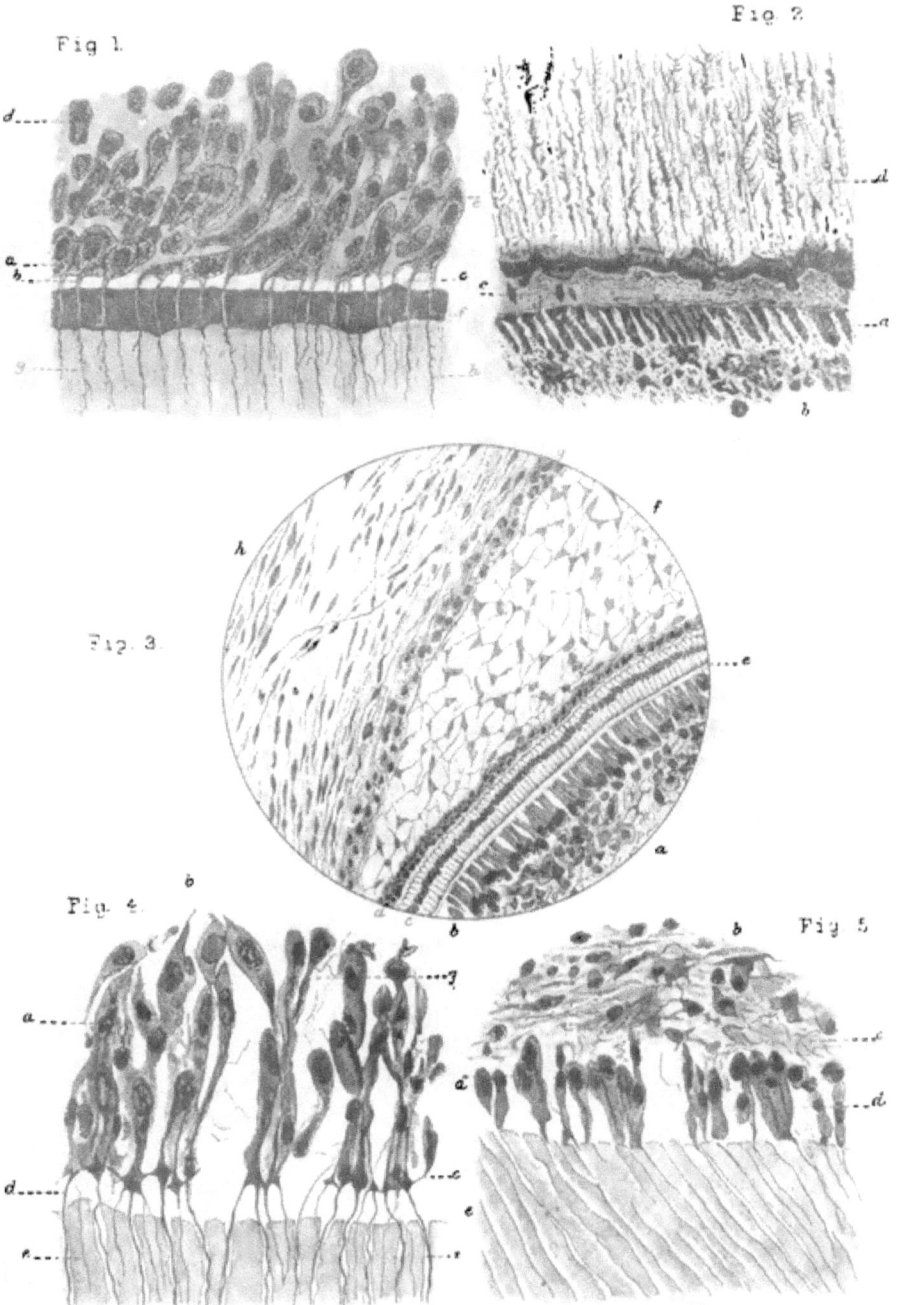

Description of Plate V.

Fig. 1.—Longitudinal section through the dentine organ of a pup at birth, hardened in Müller's fluid and alcohol: cut on a microtome: stained hæmatoxylene: ¼ in. objective and C ocular: shows (*a*) layer of odontoblast cells: (*b*) thick processes of odontoblasts at apex of dental papilla: (*c*) thin processes producing thinner fibrils: (*d*) undeveloped odontoblasts and dentogenetic cells of pulp: (*e*) homogeneous matrix in which cells are imbedded: (*f*) formed but uncalcified dentine: (*g*) calcified dentine matrix: (*h*) dentinal tubules.

Fig. 2.—Transverse section through the uncompleted apex of root of a tooth, from a photograph by Mr. Howard Mummery (*see* "Trans. Odonto. Soc.," Vol. XXII., No. 7, Plate 11, Fig. 2), × 170: prepared by Weil's process: shows (*a*) odontoblasts with square extremities: (*b*) dental pulp: (*c*) formed but uncalcified dentine, showing manner of its deposition: (*d*) dentine.

Fig. 3.—Longitudinal section through the enamel and dentine organs in the incisor region of the mandible of a fœtal pup: prepared as in Fig. 1: stained hæmatoxylene: ¼ inch and A ocular: shews (*a*) pulp: (*b*) odontoblasts: (*c*) ameloblasts: (*d*) cells of stratum intermedium: (*e*) commencement of formation of dentine and enamel: (*f*) stellate reticulum: (*g*) cells forming dental sac, its inner portion: (*h*) its outer portion.

XXII.

Fig. 4.—Transverse section of the pulp of an adult canine (human), at the broadest part of the cervical region, prepared by author's process: stained rubine: $\frac{1}{12}$ inch and C ocular: shows (*a*) odontoblasts: (*b*) their basal poles: (*c*) their median poles: (*d*) their distal processes: (*e*) dentine matrix: (*f*) dentine tubules: (*g*) fine network formed by the "supporting fibres" of the pulp.

Fig. 5.—Transverse section of same at the narrowest part of the pulp cavity: preparation and stain as above: $\frac{1}{6}$ inch and C ocular: shows (*a*) odontoblasts: (*b*) pulp: (*c*) network of fibres apparently connected with the odontoblasts: (*d*) wide intercellular spaces: (*e*) dentine.

PLATE VI.

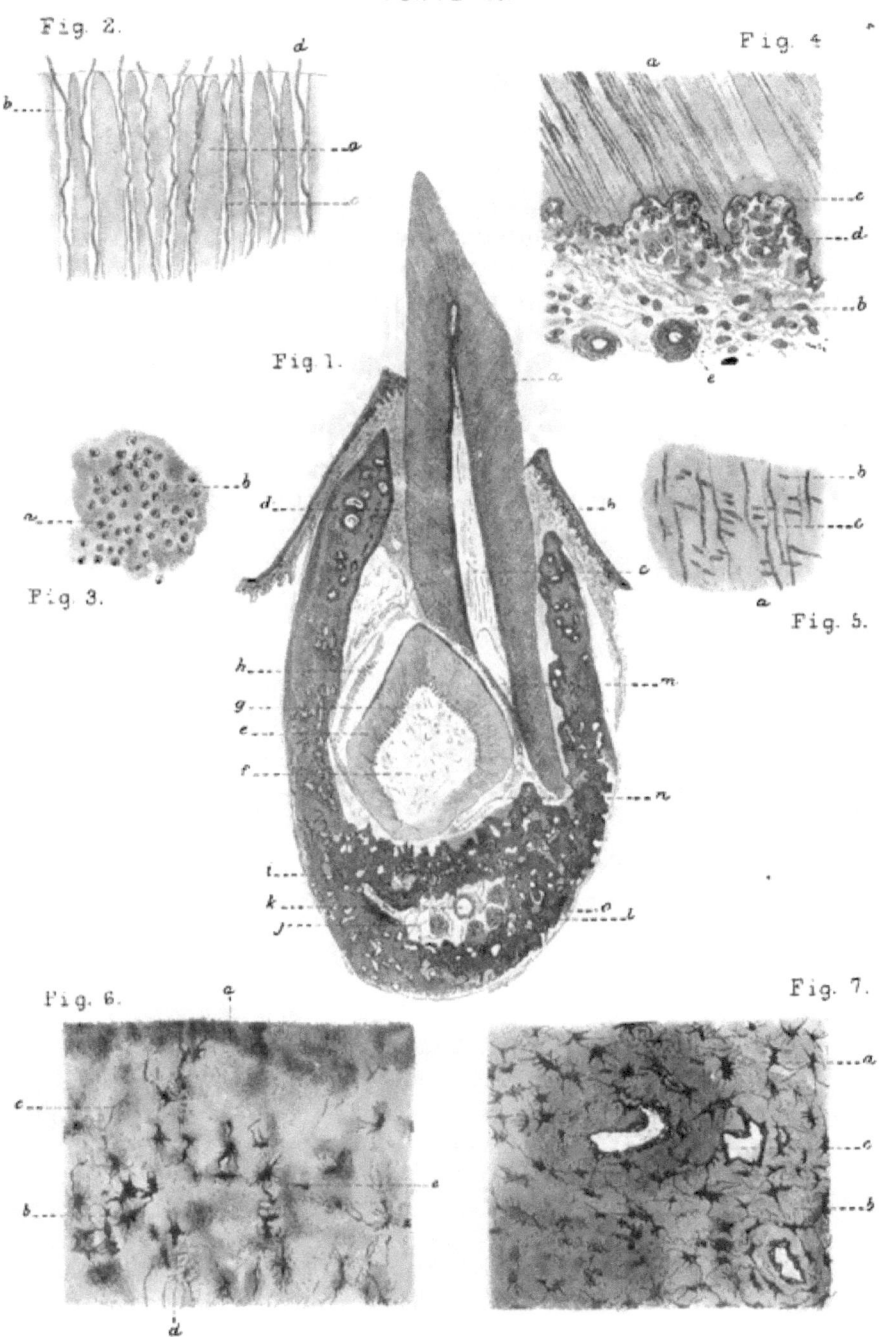

Description of Plate VI.

Fig. 1.—Vertical section of mandible of a kitten, with temporary and permanent teeth *in situ*, decalcified in chromic acid: stained carmine and methyl green: two inch objective and A ocular: shews (*a*) dentine of temporary tooth: (*b*) flange of gum: (*c*) pulp of temporary tooth: (*d*) peridental membrane: (*e*) dentine of permanent tooth: (*f*) its pulp: (*g*) odontoblast layer: (*h*) ameloblasts torn away: (*i*) bone of jaw: (*j*) inferior dental canal: (*k*) inferior dental artery: (*l*) nerve: (*m*) commencement of formation of absorbent organ: (*n*) dental sac: (*o*) alveolar periosteum.

Fig. 2.—Longitudinal section of dentine near the pulp cavity, with dentinal fibrils *in situ*: decalcified (Author's process): stained rubine: $\frac{1}{12}$ inch and C ocular: shews (*a*) dentine matrix: (*b*) tubule: (*c*) fibril: (*d*) fibril passing from pulp into tubule.

Fig. 3.—Transverse section of same: stained gold chloride: $\frac{1}{12}$ inch and C ocular: shews (*a*) tubule with fibril: (*b*) matrix.

Fig. 4.—Longitudinal section of absorbent organ *in situ*: decalcified: stained carmine: $\frac{1}{6}$ inch and A ocular: shews (*a*) dentine of temporary tooth: (*b*) absorbent organ: (*c*) Howship's lacunæ: (*d*) multi-nucleated cells: (*e*) blood vessels.

Fig. 5.—Concentric lamellæ in dentine, longitudinal section of molar (radicular portion): ground down: unstained: $\frac{1}{6}$ inch and A ocular: shews (*a*) dentine matrix; (*b*) tubule obliquely cut: (*c*) lamellæ running parallel to pulp cavity.

Fig. 6.—Transverse section of cementum, somewhat hypertrophied: ground down: stained methylene blue: ⅓ inch and A ocular: shews (*a*) structureless outer portion: (*b*) lacunæ: (*c*) canaliculi: (*d*) dentinal portion with termination of tubules: (*e*) lamellæ of cementum.

Fig. 7.—Section of alveolus of jaw, dense cancellous bone: soft parts hardened and section ground down (Caush's method): stained carmine: shews (*a*) lacunæ containing cells: (*b*) canaliculi: (*c*) spaces in cancellous bone.

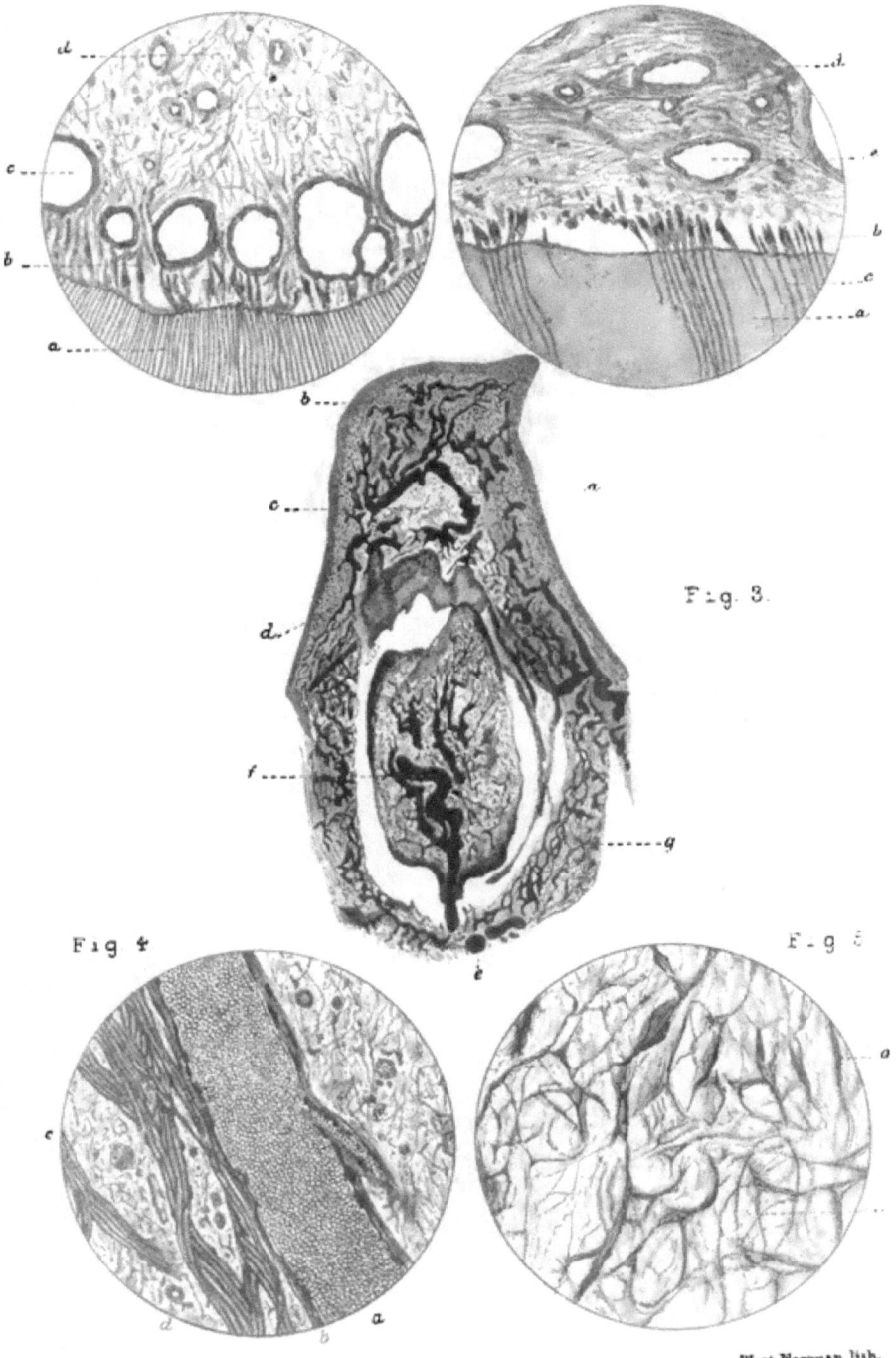

Description of Plate VII.

Fig. 1.—Transverse section of the pulp of an adult bicuspid (human), at the broadest part of the extreme radicular region of the tooth; prepared by the author's process: stained hæmatoxylene: $\frac{1}{8}$ inch objective and A ocular: shews (*a*) dentine: (*b*) the insignificant nature of the odontoblasts: (*c*) large capillaries at the periphery of the pulp: (*d*) pulp tissue.

Fig. 2.—Longitudinal section of the pulp of an adult canine (human) at the apex of the radicular region; author's process: stained rubine: $\frac{1}{8}$ inch and A ocular: shews (*a*) dentine: (*b*) insignificant odontoblasts: (*c*) tubules corresponding in direction with the long axes of the odontoblasts and coincidence of absence of both: (*d*) pulp tissue: (*e*) capillary, obliquely cut.

Fig. 3.—Vertical section of the mandible of a fœtal kitten, injected to shew the vascular supply, hardened in Müller's fluid and alcohol: general tissues stained carmine, vessels injected with Prussian blue: 2 inch and A ocular: shews (*a*) external set of capillaries, supplying: (*b*) gum, (*c*) enamel organ, and (*d*) ameloblasts: (*e*) internal set, supplying (*f*) pulp, and (*g*) various peridental tissues.

Fig. 4.—Longitudinal section of the dental pulp, hardened in Müller's fluid: stained chloride of gold: $\frac{1}{8}$ inch and A ocular: shews (*a*) capillary filled with blood corpuscles: (*b*) capillary wall: (*c*) bundles of nerve fibres: (*d*) pulp tissue.

Fig. 5.—Fibrous stroma of pulp from temporary tooth of a monkey: hardened in perchloride of mercury and alcohol: stained carmine: $\frac{1}{8}$ inch and A ocular: shews (*a*) large fibres: (*b*) delicate reticulum of fine "supporting fibres."

PLATE VIII.

Fig. 1.

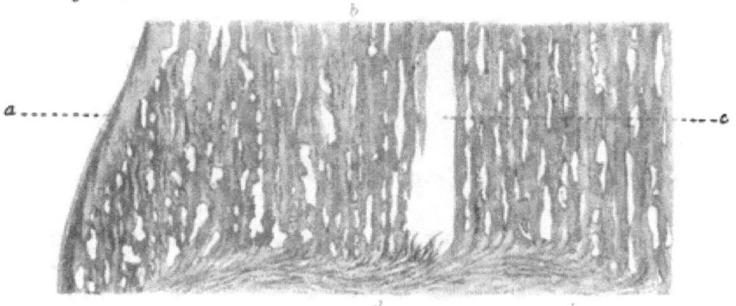

Fig. 2.

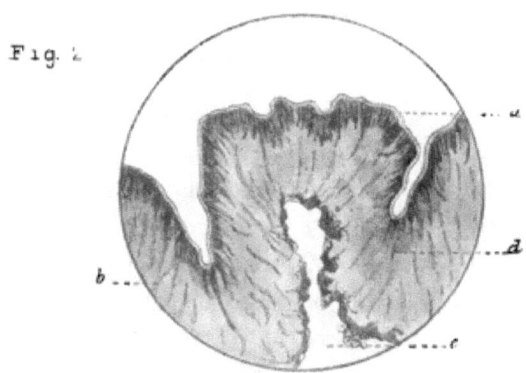

Fig. 3.

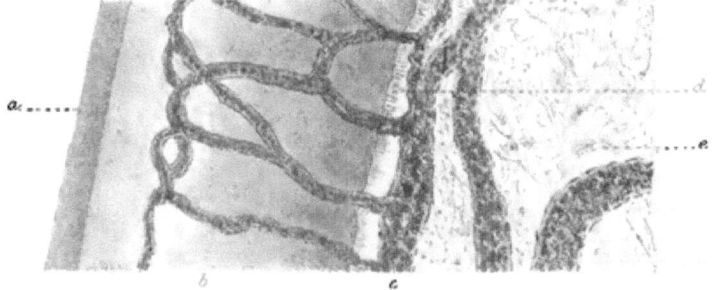

Description of Plate VIII.

Fig. 1.—This and the accompanying figures are intended to shew three of the chief varieties of dentine. *Osteo-dentine.*—Longitudinal section of an anchylosed tooth of the pike (Esox lucius), decalcified: stained carmine: 1 inch objective and A ocular: shews (*a*) free surface of dentine: (*b*) osteo-dentine: (*c*) inter-trabecular spaces: (*d*) bone of attachment.

Fig. 2.—*Plici-dentine.*—Transverse section of a tooth of the basking shark (Selache maxima), decalcified: stained carmine: 2 inch and A ocular: shews (*a*) folded free surface of tooth: (*b*) large tubes: (*c*) pulp chamber, soft tissues not retained: (*d*) plici-dentine.

Fig. 3.—*Vaso-dentine.*—Longitudinal section of a tooth of the hake (Gadus merlucius), prepared by the author's process: stained picro-carmine: $\frac{1}{4}$ inch and A ocular: shews (*a*) free surface of tooth: (*b*) vaso-dentine: (*c*) naturally injected capillaries traversing canals in dentine (Tomes' thorn-like processes of canals not shown): (*d*) layer of connective tissue fibre bundles: (*e*) pulp tissue.

DENTAL MICROSCOPY.

CHAPTER I.

INTRODUCTORY.

Introduction

THE non-existence of a treatise on Dental Microscopy may be safely advanced as an excuse for the Author's presentation of the following pages. He has been induced to give publicity to his work with the microscope in this special branch of science, practical instruction and hints in manipulation being his main object.

It is interesting to observe how rapidly this scientific dental work has of late years advanced, and how many of the younger members of the profession are taking it up. By the establishment of special classes for Dental Histology, at the various schools; by a much needed examination, in this subject, at the termination of the student's curriculum; and, by the wide fields of research still open to the original worker, it will be readily seen, that we have to deal with a question of no mean importance. This fact is now recognised by the members of the

---

NOTE.—The drawings throughout this work are made, for the most part, from original photographs.

British Dental Association, at whose Annual Meetings, papers, demonstrations, and discussions form an interesting and valuable feature.

Reasons for Publication.

The Manuals of General Histology, which are present day text-books, refer but very briefly to this special subject: mere outlines of practical work are, as a rule, only given, the demonstrators, at the schools, adopting in class their own methods of carrying out the rules there laid down. With a view, therefore, of helping dental students in their work, it is the writer's desire, to place on record the details of those methods, chiefly in vogue at the present time, which he has found of greatest use; thereby hoping to stimulate individual work at home, as an addition to that of the hospital practical class. The notes will be didactic, helpful, and instructive. No attempts will be made to teach Dental Histology: students must rely, for this purpose, on their own lecturers and text-books.

The Illustrations.

These pages, however, are accompanied by original illustrations, drawn by the author from his own preparations, and instructions are given as to the methods recommended for making such specimens. The plates are thus intended to be a useful feature, and a help to the student. A short description will be found accompanying each plate, in order that he, who has prepared and mounted a section, may be able, under the microscope, to recognise its various structures, and seeing, learn and interpret its meaning. He will thus become familiar with his own sections, and by comparison with those of others, quickly understand the broad facts of Dental Histology.

General Remarks.

As with everything that requires for its proper performance the application of technical manipulative skill in addition to complete fore-knowledge of the subject, so it is with Dental Microscopy. It is essentially made up of minutiæ; it is a matter of much detail; and the student must begin at the very beginning, if he wishes to become a microscopist and histologist. Many difficulties will necessarily arise at first, but experience and practice will, in time, lead the diligent enquirer to successful and gratifying achievements.

The simpler the apparatus he employs, the better; the less complicated the method he adopts, the truer the results.

The Microscope.—A simple form of compound microscope should be used at the commencement of histological studies, this being more suitable, firstly, because of the ease of management, and secondly, because it involves no great initial outlay. The shape, or size of stand, is immaterial, it should be heavy and quite firm: the objectives must, however, be good. These should be, for ordinary purposes, 1 inch and $\frac{1}{6}$ inch, which, with two eye-pieces—"A" and "C" or "D," as they are usually called—give a magnification ranging variously from 35 to 750 diameters. Later on, a $\frac{1}{12}$ inch, water or oil immersion, will be found indispensable for the examination of bacteria and for fine work generally. The microscope should be provided with rack and pinion or "coarse," and screw, or "fine" adjustments, and a reversible mirror. It is advisable to have a double nose-piece attached to the draw tube, much time and trouble being thus saved. This accessory is not, however, quite essential at first, and a mechanical stage need not be purchased until later. A sub-stage with focussing and swinging adjustments, an Abbé condenser, iris diaphragm, and bull's-eye condenser, on stand, make up the necessary primary equipments. The student should obtain catalogues

Instruments.

The Objectives.

Makers of Microscopes. of the various instrument makers and dealers, among whom may be mentioned Messrs. Baker of Holborn, Beck of Cornhill, Powell and Lealand of Euston Road, Steward of Strand, Swift of Tottenham Court Road, Watson of Holborn, Frazer of Edinburgh, and Parke of Birmingham. It is invidious to make distinctions, but the writer can specially recommend Beck's "Star" microscope as being eminently suited, at first, for all the requirements of the student. It is a cheap form of instrument, but the objectives are certainly very good.

Fig. 1.

THE "STAR" MICROSCOPE

Fig. 2.

SWIFT'S FOUR-LEGGED MICROSCOPE.

Use of Parts of Microscopes

The various parts of a microscope can be more readily understood by reference to the accompanying drawing than by a long verbal description.

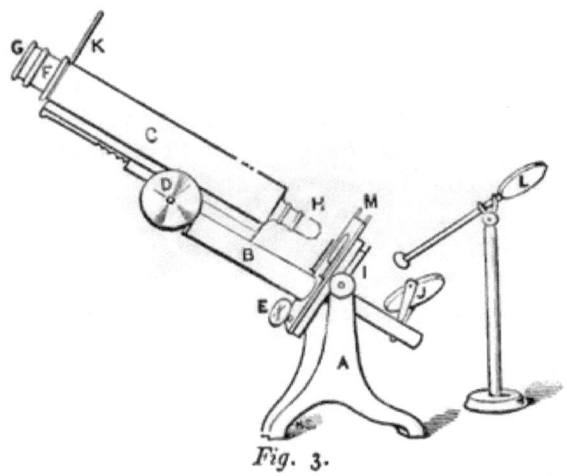

Fig. 3.

THE PARTS OF A MICROSCOPE.

A. Foot or stand of microscope.
B. Limb.
C. Body.
D. Coarse adjustment.
E. Fine adjustment.
F. Draw tube.
G. Eye-piece or ocular.
H. Objective lens.

I. Sub-stage with Abbé condenser.
J. Reversible mirror carried by tail-piece.
K. Screen mentioned in text (moved aside).
L. Bull's-eye condenser.
M. The stage.

The uses and actions of these parts are briefly as follows :—

Foot.

The *Foot* supports the microscope, and keeps it rigid and fixed in one position. It should be heavy and firm, and the form shown in the drawing, known as the Jackson, is the best, for it allows the instrument to be placed in a horizontal position without losing its firmness and support.

The *Limb* is very solid. It sometimes carries, *Limb.*
at the end furthest from the foot, the fine adjustment.

The *Body* is the optical tube through which the *Body.*
objects are seen. It is provided at one end with the
objective, and at the other with the *Draw-Tube,*
which accurately fits its interior. It is attached to
the limb by means of a rack and pinion adjustment.
Some cheap forms of microscope have no rack and
pinion, but for convenience and usefulness, this is
really necessary.

The *Objectives* and *Eye-Pieces* are the magnifiers, *Objectives and*
and the magnification of the object depends on these *Eye-Pieces.*
only, and not on the size of the stand of the microscope,
as is sometimes supposed. The powers of the former
are expressed as 1 inch, $\frac{1}{4}$ inch, etc. These terms do
not indicate the distance at which they focus on the
object, but mean the actual magnifying power of the
objective. Thus, a 1 inch objective should have a
power of 10 diameters, $\frac{1}{6}$ inch 60, and so on. The
ocular again amplifies the image formed by the
objective, 3, 5, or more times.

The *Coarse Adjustment* raises and lowers the body, *The Adjust-*
and is required for focussing with the lower powers. *ments*
The *Fine Adjustment* is to be used with higher powers
for very delicately focussing. The *Sub-Stage* carries *Sub-Stage*
the illuminating apparatus, Abbé condenser, and *and Dia-*
diaphragms for concentrating the light on to the *phragms.*
object. The function of the diaphragms is to cut
off circumfluent rays of light, and make the image
well defined and bright.

The *Plane Mirror* is used for low powers by *Mirrors*
daylight and with the condenser. The *Concave*
is employed when a maximum amount of light
is required, and for high powers by lamp-light.

The *Stage* holds the glass slide in position by *Stage*
means of clips.

Condenser. The *Bull's-Eye Condenser* is necessary for condensing light on opaque objects, and for photo-micrography.

Screen. A useful adjunct to the microscope is a home-made *Screen* for protecting the eye. It should be a dull-black piece of carboard, 2 inches by 4¾, in which a circle has been made towards one end, to slip over the draw-tube. When in position (see fig. 2), the unoccupied eye can remain open, and much comfort, with no fatigue of vision will thus be assured. The dark back-ground renders the image, through the microscope lens, free from all extraneous objects lying on the table top. Both eyes remain open, one being, of course, used for viewing the object.

Apparatus required. The room for work should be well lighted, and should contain a firm table and cupboard.

Mr. J. Mansbridge's List. Appended is a list of instruments suggested by the Histology Demonstrator (Mr. J. Mansbridge), at Guy's Hospital Dental School, and used by the students in that Institution:

A COMPOUND MICROSCOPE.—NOTE.—The instrument should have a firm stand, and be fitted with rack and pinion, coarse and fine adjustments, and an "Indicator."

The OBJECTIVES should be well "corrected," and have good penetrating power, with flatness of field.

A double NOSE-PIECE.

PINE-WOOD box to hold six dozen slides, lying flat.

Six dozen or more GLASS SLIPS, 3 × 1 inch, ground edges.

Half-ounce thin COVER GLASSES, ¾-inch diameter, circular.

One-eighth ounce thin COVER GLASSES, 1¼ × ⅜ inch, oval or oblong.

INTRODUCTORY.

Forceps and needles, set in handles.
Camels' hair Brushes, 2 large and 2 small.
Small pair of Scissors, 2 section lifters.
Three sizes glass Capsules, with glass lids.
Small glass Funnel and filter papers.
Half-dozen deep Watch Glasses.
Hot Table, 6 in. high, the top 4 in. square.
Small Spirit Lamp, to go under same.
Half-dozen Clips.
An Arkansas and an oil Stone.
One box of neat square Labels.
A silk Handkerchief.

The above are those instruments generally used in class work. In addition, may be mentioned for private use:— *Additions to List.*

A good microscope Lamp.
An ether freezing Microtome.
Two or three large Stone Jars, corked.
Stoppered glass Bottles of 2 oz., 4 oz., and 8 oz. capacities.
A Rack containing half-a-dozen Wolrab gold cylinder bottles (fig. 4).

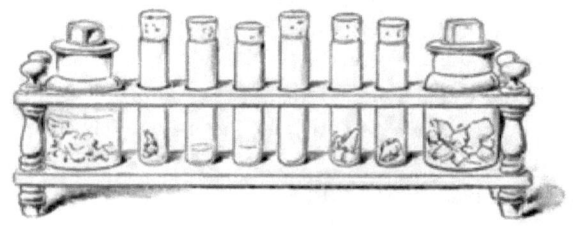

Fig. 4.

RACK FOR HOLDING BOTTLES,
CONTAINING SPECIMENS, &c.

A small glass Pipette, fitted with india-rubber suction tube.
Glass Measure, divided into cubic-centimetres.

Two section LIFTERS, one large and one small, made of aluminium or bone (for using with acid solutions).

A TURN-TABLE for "ringing" slides.

Small dissecting FORCEPS and SCALPEL.

The slides should be as thin and flat as possible, have rounded edges, and be free from scratches.

About Cover Glasses.

The cover-glasses should be the thinnest (·004) procurable. Circles are more useful than squares, except in a few cases, because they are easily "rung" after the section has been mounted. They should be kept in cotton wool in a small box, and wiped carefully with a silk handkerchief, flat on the table, or between the fingers. Some workers prefer to keep them in a jar of water acidulated with nitric acid. The objectives and eye-pieces should always be cleaned by means of a small piece of soft wash-leather, both before and after using, and the microscope kept, when not wanted, under a glass shade.

The nose-piece is a useful addition to the microscope. It is better for the student to purchase one made of aluminium rather than brass. For, after some years, it will be found that the fine adjustment gets a little out of order, in consequence of the extra weight on the body and draw-tube of the instrument.

Method of using the Microscope.

To those students, who are quite beginners and have never handled a microscope, the following remarks may be of service:—

The Question of Light.

The instrument having been placed on a firm table, near a window facing N. or W. in the morning, S. or E., in the afternoon, out of the rays of direct sunlight, it should be tilted to a convenient angle, the student being seated. The 1-inch objective, and "A" or No. 1 ocular in place, and the specimen fixed firmly on the stage by means of the clips, the plane mirror is now to be moved, in such a manner, that a flood of light passes through the aperture of the stage, and illuminates, equally, in all parts, the section to be examined. It is advisable to make sure of this by looking at the stage and section, not through the microscope tube at all, but at the side of the instrument. No diaphragm is to be used for the low powers. The coarse adjustment must now be carefully screwed up or down, as the case may be, until the specimen is seen to be in focus. If this has been done, as just described, the field of vision will be equally bright and clear, and the image sharp, but reversed. Every part of the section should be examined, by moving the slide about, using for this purpose the fingers of both hands to steady it. With Beck's 1-inch objective and "A" ocular, thus, the magnification—an important point in histological work—will be about 35, and, if "C" ocular is substituted for the lower power, the magnification equals 90 diameters. *Examination of Specimen.*

If it is the wish of the observer to examine more minutely any particular part of the section, he should place that in the centre of the field. The ¼-inch objective is then moved or screwed into position, after having first screwed up the coarse adjustment as far as possible, to prevent all risk of breaking the cover-glass or damaging the lens. If "A" ocular is used, and the plane changed for the concave mirror (care being again taken to equally illuminate the field of vision by means of the condenser and a small diaphragm), the coarse adjustment should bring the objective close to, but not touching the cover-glass, the fine adjustment being finally used for focussing. The magnification is now nearly 200. When "A" ocular is removed and "C" takes its place, the magnification *To get a higher Magnification* exceeds 510. To get a still higher magnification, the draw-tube of the microscope may be extended one, two or three inches. If it is thus lengthened, the section will be magnified 750 times.

Choice of Powers.

The student, however, should be satisfied with using only, for many weeks, the low power objective and eye-piece. Later on, he can combine them with the higher powers, and produce the various magnifications obtainable. That the employment of

Low Powers. low powers for ordinary work is the best, may be well conceived, when it is remembered that a clear steady illumination is produced by simple means, that the precision of the focal adjustment is not of the greatest consequence, and that the tendency towards errors of refraction of light is considerably lessened. A large field of vision is presented, and the position that cells and other structures occupy, with regard to the surrounding tissues, their relative size and number, and general characteristics are all best observed under a low amplification.

High Powers. With high powers, the minute anatomy of the tissues—the markings of cells, structure of their walls, etc.—is brought out; but, *per contra*, the object is less defined, the illumination considerably reduced, and there is greater fear of spherical and chromatic aberration, leading to distortion and a false appearance of the image.

It will be some time before the beginner can manipulate the sub-stage condenser in a satisfactory manner. It is unnecessary to add a long account of it, experience in its use, as throughout microscopy, is by far the best instructor.

The above is the plan for viewing transparent objects by daylight or lamplight, opaque specimens being seldom, if ever, used in dental work.

Preliminary Exercise.

The student having by this time become well acquainted with the various parts of the microscope, their functions and movements, should proceed to follow the good advice given by Schäfer in his "Essentials of Histology." He should make temporary slides of the common objects of his room, e.g., dust, fibres of cotton, silk, etc., and also mount a few air-bubbles. By so doing, he will be spared much trouble, annoyance, and loss of time. But the golden rule in Practical Microscopy, is to thoroughly learn to use the low powers, before work with $\frac{1}{6}$ or $\frac{1}{12}$ inch objectives is attempted.

As before mentioned, each chapter will contain the methods of preparing sections of histological specimens. If the instructions, there given, are carefully followed, the student will, by using the objectives and oculars indicated, and by comparing the sections he has made, be enabled to see, on the stage of his own microscope, images almost identical with those, figured on the plates. *Practical Examples.*

Thus, a human tooth having been prepared, according to the plans detailed in the following chapter, is mounted and examined with $\frac{1}{6}$ in. objective and "A" eye-piece. The student will observe, through his own instrument, appearances similar to those found in Plate I, Fig. 1. He should compare the drawing with the actual preparation, and, although the former will generally be somewhat diagrammatic—for the sake of clearness—he will soon be able to readily recognize the most prominent features of his own slide. In connection with each figure, the methods of preparation, the stain, and the magnifying powers used are mentioned, and the salient histological structure of the section brought out.

CHAPTER II.

On the Preparation of the Hard Tissues.

At the outset of practical Dental Microscopy, it must be clearly understood by the student, that, having mastered all the details of the management of a microscope, it is of the highest importance, in the preparation of tissues for histological purposes, to treat his specimens, both chemically and mechanically, in such a manner that their structures will be altered as little as possible. It is a very great question whether or not one ever sees through the microscope tissues which are not somewhat changed in appearance, either by swelling or shrinkage. The student's aim, therefore, is to prepare sections free from these defects, and the employment of fresh materials, re-agents, and reliable processes, cannot be too strongly insisted upon.

General Principles.

Grinding down Hard Tissues. Advantages and Disadvantages.

There are two chief principles of treatment to be adopted when preparing the hard dental tissues for microscopical examination and research, and each, in its own way, answers the purpose admirably. These are :—(A) RUBBING or GRINDING DOWN the tissue in its hard calcified state. (B) CUTTING BY MICROTOME after decalcification.

A.

The former is the older and more general method. For many years it has been a favourite with histologists, but it possesses several serious drawbacks. Broken-down detritus, dust, and air, get into and are retained in the interspaces, and though the sections shew degrees of contrast well, they are very much spoilt if extraneous matters are also present. It is difficult, too, to get a portion of tooth thin enough for examination with the higher powers. Very often pieces of the part to be preserved, break in a most disappointing fashion at the last moment, and the work of hours is thereby rendered useless. Ground-down sections take stains badly, as a rule; that is to say, the colouring matter penetrates the parts somewhat imperfectly. Only two or three specimens can be obtained from one tooth, and sometimes it is necessary, when investigating matters, to make sections from a single specimen, in transverse, horizontal, and in vertical directions. This can easily be done if the tissue be decalcified, but only with very great difficulty if the simple grinding-down process is adopted. It must also be remembered that such mechanical manipulations are at times tedious, irksome and lengthy. Still, the method of grinding-down must not be considered by any means obsolete. The structure of the hard parts is well retained and exhibited.

The following are the chief methods employed :— *Various Methods.*

(1) *Grinding-down Sections of Hard Tissues on a Wheel.*

The tissue is held by means of the finger tips on the right hand side of a vertical, rapidly revolving, sharp, dry corundum or carborundum wheel, until a perfectly flat surface results. Great care must be taken, for, if the wheel revolves too rapidly, the tooth will probably be cracked or broken. Much heat and a smell of burning dentine are evolved, which make it rather unpleasant. The flat surface is now rubbed down on a dry Arkansas stone, and finally, to remove all scratches, polished on a razor strop, also used dry. The finished side is then fastened on to a piece of thick glass—a microscope slide will do—with hard Canada balsam, which has been previously warmed and softened over a spirit lamp. After the balsam has cooled a little, the

Charters White's Method Modified.

The Dry Method.

polished tooth surface is pressed into it, flat on to the glass, and allowed to remain there. When the balsam is set hard, which, in practice, may take some days, the exposed surface of tooth may be ground and polished in the same way. The tooth is then ready for mounting.* Soluble glass (silicate of soda) with hydrate of sodium may be used, and is even preferable to Canada balsam for fastening the specimen on the slide. A drop is placed on a slide, and the polished surface of the section pressed on to it. In a few hours the slice of tooth is quite firmly fixed, and grinding and polishing can be proceeded with at once. Thus, much saving of time is effected. Care must be taken to avoid wetting the specimen, as water dissolves soluble glass. Resin and wax (3 to 1) may be also substituted for the above media. It will be noticed that everything here is done in a dry condition, and a mere skeleton of the tooth remains.

Mr. Charters White, who originally introduced this plan in 1885,† recommended the use of a wet buff leather, with putty powder sprinkled on it, but the above mentioned method is perhaps better.

(2) *Rubbing Down Between Plates of Glass.*

The Wet Method.

Slices of the hard portions of a tooth are cut under dripping water with a fine fret-saw. If it is sharp it easily cuts dentine. The enamel being extremely hard, will require notching previously with a very thin corundum wheel.

If it is not desired to make more than one section from the same specimen (*e.g.* the lower jaw of a rat with teeth *in situ*), it saves time to do the preliminary grinding under water, on a corundum wheel. In this case the tissue need not be fixed by balsam on

---

* The Methods of Mounting will be found on page 76.

† Transactions of British Dental Association, Annual Meeting, 1885.

to glass, but should be ground down on both sides, the fingers holding it on the wheel.

Place a slice of the specimen between two plates of ground glass, their dull sides meeting. It is convenient to have the lower plate the larger of the two, 18-20 inches square. The upper should be 10-15 inches square. On the top of the tooth pour a little water, and add a small amount of the finest pumice powder. With a rotary movement of the upper glass, rub down the section till it is thin. Towards the end of the process, carefully watch the section through the upper glass, using no pumice, but plenty of water. Old and worn ground-glass plates are useful for polishing already thinned sections, and should be kept for this purpose. When the section is quite transparent, remove it from the glass carefully with the fingers, or a pair of fine forceps, wash in water, and then place it in a bottle of alcohol, till the time has come to mount it.*

The following modifications have recently been introduced :—

Mr. Dunkerley ("Journal Royal Microscopical Society," part 6, 1892) proceeds as follows :— *Dunkerley's Method.*

"Sections are cut off the tooth, by means of a thin copper disc, fitted to a dental lathe, and revolving in a trough containing water and fine corundum powder. The thin disc is now replaced by a thick one, with the same trough and contents. The sides of this disc are used as a lapidary's stone to grind these sections thinner, one side of which is next polished on Water of Ayr stone, under running water, this surface being afterwards secured to a glass slip by thick Canada balsam. The grinding of the section on the thick copper disc is now proceeded with, until the section is thin enough to

---

* In connection with this, the student is referred to Mr. Charters White's work on "The Microscope and How to Use It," 1893, pp. 38-42.

see the structure; then proceed to polish this surface on the Water of Ayr stone, until all details are visible under the microscope, when, after careful washing, the section is mounted."

The plan seems well adopted for cutting sections of specially large teeth, *e.g.*, molars of horse, elephant, etc.

J. J. Andrew's Method.

Mr. J. J. Andrew's Plan:—The tooth to be ground is cut into as fine a slice as possible, by the aid of small saws. It is then reduced in thickness by grinding on a corundum wheel on the lathe, a copious supply of water being allowed meanwhile to flow over the section. The finger presses it carefully against the wheel, until it is very nearly thin enough for microscopic examination. It is finally ground between a couple of fine soft hones, made of Hindostan or other stone of similar fineness of grit, finishing to remove scratches between two Arkansas hones. The section is then well washed, the water dried off between the folds of fine blotting paper, and mounted in Canada Balsam.

Whittles' Lathe

Mr. Dencer Whittles recently exhibited a lathe, which he has devised, for carrying stones for grinding-down purposes. It is placed on end and mounted on a table. The wheels revolve horizontally, in this case, the motor power being produced by the lathe band passing over pulleys which are placed at right angles to the treadle wheel. This arrangement will prove very useful for the final grinding and polishing of sections that have been prepared by Weil's process.

B.

Decalcification of Hard Tissues. Advantages and Disadvantages.

Decalcification of the Hard Tissues.

It has been the fashion of late to decry the use of acids for decalcifying purposes, but rapid softening, which the writer strongly upholds, seems quite satisfactory. It is true, that one cannot tell the precise chemical actions that occur when an acid is brought into contact with dentine or enamel: it is true, that it appears to be destructive to the tissues, and, it must be confessed, changes them somewhat, but, given the immense advantages accruing from its use, it will be found, that, as a rule, more instruction can be gained from decalcified sections than from those ground or rubbed down. To briefly mention these advantages, it may be said, that the sections are much thinner than those of non-decalcified teeth. Any number can be obtained from one and the same tooth. They stain well, and can be rendered very transparent. It is also, more easy to cut them, while the trouble of preparation is reduced to a minimum.

There are many decalcifying fluids and acids now used in histological work, the best known being, hydrochloric, nitric, picric, chromic, acetic, and arsenic acids. The prolonged immersion of a tooth in commercial glycerine softens and removes the lime salts; but it is not used for decalcifying purposes, unless combined with hydrochloric acid in the proportion of glycerine 95 and acid 5 parts. The mixture acts slowly, too slowly almost, but preserves specimens while it softens them. It possesses the merit that it does not seem to blur or destroy the structure of dentine or cementum. *Decalcifying Agents.*

These decalcifying agents are here enumerated in the order of their importance and usefulness in Dental Microscopy. Their strengths vary considerably; thus, hydrochloric acid is most useful when made up to a 10 per cent. solution, picric—a cold saturated aqueous solution, and nitric and chromic, in one per cent. solutions. The last named acid is also particularly serviceable in a crystalline form. Strong solutions are recommended in preference to weak ones. It is a rule, with but few exceptions, that the after-effects of the acid should be neutralized by immersion in an alkaline fluid. Bicarbonate of soda, one dram to one pint of water, is perhaps the most convenient.

Acids.   All acid solutions must be perfectly fresh and kept in glass-stoppered bottles, wooden instruments and aluminium or plated section lifters being used in manipulating the tissues.

It is very advisable to employ a fixed quantity of acid solution in decalcifying teeth and bone. The writer finds that twelve c.c., or four fluid drachms is a good quantity to use. The bottles used by Wolrab for packing gold cylinders will easily contain the amount.* This rule applies chiefly to the hydrochloric acid solutions. By using this fixed quantity, the exact strength is known, and the probable length of time required for softening can be readily ascertained. The bottle should bear a small label, on which are noted the kind of specimen, the name of the solution in which it is immersed, and the date of immersion, to be followed by another small label, giving details of times of changing the solutions.

But, after all, the proper strength and periods of time for immersion can best be learnt by experience, because they depend, not only on the size of the tissue, but on its quality and structure. No hard and fast rules can be laid down.

Other Methods of Decalcification.

Dr. Black, in "Periosteum and Peridental Membrane," speaks of using a 3 % solution of nitric acid. He remarks:—"It has been found that the element of time is . . . . more important than the strength of the acid solution employed."

---

* This is a form of corked sample bottle.

Bödecker * has been able to make specimens of teeth provided with *all* the hard tissues, by first grinding fresh teeth on a corundum wheel, and then decalcifying the thin section, in a large quantity of a ½ per cent. solution of chromic acid, for one or two days. Dilute glycerine is the solvent.

Decalcifying Methods.

Ebner's decalcifying fluid consists of:—

        H Cl.   1 gramme.
        Na. Cl.   10 grammes.
        Water to 100 c.c.

This is a useful formula, but great quantities of the solution must be used, and it should be quite fresh.†

Hart, of New York,‡ divides a tooth into several pieces and immerses them after they have been ground thin, in a six per cent. solution of glacial acetic acid. Here they remain for ten hours, and are subsequently treated in the ordinary way.

Kleinenberg's formula is:—

Saturated aqueous solution of picric acid   100 parts.
Strong sulphuric acid   ...   .   2 ,,
Filter and add, distilled water ...   ...   300 ,,

Lepkowski § suggests the sub-joined method for preparing sections of dentine, which possesses the advantages of simultaneously softening and staining it.

Pieces of teeth, which should be no thicker than ½ m.m., are placed in a solution made of pure formic acid 3 parts, and 1 per cent. aqueous solution of gold chloride, 6 parts. They remain here for twenty-four hours, are then removed, washed with distilled water,

---

* Heitzmann's "Microscopical Morphology of the Animal Body," 1884, page 613.
† Crookshank's "Practical Bacteriology," 1890, page 25.
‡ "Dental Cosmos," September, 1891.
§ "Journal British Dental Association," Vol. XIV., p. 248.

and placed in a mixture of gum arabic and glycerine for twenty-four hours. On removal, they are again washed in distilled water, then alcohol, and finally imbedded in celloidin or paraffin.

The following are good methods for the preparation of specimens for the

Demonstration of Special Hard Tissues.

To show Enamel Fibres.

Enamel Fibres can be prepared by immersing a tooth in 12 c.c. of a 10 per cent. solution of hydrochloric acid. At the end of thirty hours, on removal from the acid, the enamel will be quite soft. A small portion should be taken up with a needle, or brush, and placed on a slide. The mass should then be teased out with needle points, and a drop of normal salt solution placed on the top, and a cover-glass applied. The staining is effected by allowing a solution of carmine or rubine to run beneath the cover-glass by capillary attraction. Excess of stain can be removed by blotting paper, and further washed away by irrigation with water acidulated with one per cent. acetic acid, and in this or in salt solution, the enamel prisms are mounted (Plate 1, Fig. 2). It is important to "ring" the cover-glass as soon afterwards as practicable.

Nasmyth's Membrane.

Nasmyth's Membrane.—Immerse a permanent human tooth, by preference a newly erupted one, (although the membrane persists over all, even old teeth), in a 10 per cent. solution of hydrochloric acid. In two and a half hours the membrane will begin to be separated from the surface of the enamel, and can soon be removed by means of a wooden needle-like point or brush. It should be washed in alkaline solution, then in water, and finally kept in rectified spirits of wine for further treatment (Plate 1, Fig. 5). Sections of Nasmyth's membrane, *in situ*, may be obtained by first grinding down a tooth, as already described, placing it on a slide, and putting over it a cover-glass. If the hydrochloric acid solution be now run underneath the cover-glass, in a few hours the membrane will become detached from the free edge of enamel, and afterwards can be permanently mounted.

The Sheaths of Neumann. (Plate II., Fig. 2.) Break a tooth into four or five pieces in a vice, and place the fragments in a 10 per cent. solution of hydrochloric acid. At the end of three days, change the acid. At the end of five days, add 5 c.c. of pure nitric acid. At the end of seven days, remove the pieces from the solution. Transfer the soft mucoid deposit, which has collected at the bottom of the Wolrab bottle, to a glass slide, and teare it out with needle points, after a drop of distilled water has been placed over it. Press down a cover-glass, and stain with borax or lithium carmine, which should be allowed to run underneath, as first described.

Sheaths of Neumann.

The sheaths are thus isolated, and very similar in appearance to yellow elastic connective tissue fibres.

To Shew Dentine and Cementum. (1) Take a newly extracted tooth (human) and place it in a solution of

Dentine and Cementum.

    Chromic acid (crystals)   10 grains.
    Water   8 ounces.

It should remain here for two days, at the end of which time, a fresh solution should be used.

(2) Then immerse it in a solution of

    Chromic acid   20 grains.
    Water   8 ounces.

for four days.

(3) Finally, place the tooth in

Chromic acid	20 grains.
Water	4 ounces.
Hydrochloric acid (2¼ per cent. sol.)	4 ounces.

The latter should be added about ten minutes after the chromic acid solution is made.

(4) Remove the tissue to fresh solutions made up according to the last formula, every fourth day, until it is sufficiently soft (eleven or twelve days).

By using the chromic acid as mentioned, the advantages derived from the employment of fresh agents are assured.

Wash the tooth for twelve hours under running water, after it has been immersed for half-an-hour in an alkaline solution.

Another Method.

Another and more usual method for efficiently showing the structure of enamel, dentine, and and cementum, is to make a vertical section of an adult human tooth, by first grinding down on a wheel, and then between plates of glass, finally mounting the section, unstained, in Canada balsam.

Laminæ

Laminæ in Dentine can be demonstrated by adopting Mr. F. J. Bennett's glycerine methods.*

These are briefly the following:—

(*a*) Freshly extracted teeth are ground down until very thin. The sections are then polished, and suspended in pure glycerine, or glycerine and bicarbonate of soda, for one to six months. Then they are washed and mounted in glycerine; or,

(*b*) Freshly extracted teeth are immersed whole in pure glycerine for a similar period. Then ground down, polished, and mounted; or,

---

*See "Transactions, Odontological Society of Great Britain," November, 1888.

(c) Whole teeth are placed in a very diluted solution of glycerine, whose strength is daily increased until pure glycerine is used. Then they are kept in this for one to two months, and treated as in (b).

The structure of *Cementum, Interglobular Spaces, Striæ of Retzius, Owen's* and *Schreger's lines* are all best demonstrated by grinding-down and polishing, and, generally speaking, leaving the tissue unstained. *Cementum, etc.*

Fish's Teeth and Jaws of Animals can be prepared by either grinding-down or decalcifying them. Small teeth and jaws are difficult to grind down, and sections are therefore better prepared by immersion in acid, *viz.*, either a 5 per cent. solution of chromic acid, or 10 per cent. of hydrochloric acid, and after washing and neutralization, impregnation with gum or paraffin prior to their cutting on a microtome. *Fish's Teeth.*

Table of Hard Tissues suitable for Preparation by

Grinding or Rubbing Down.	Decalcification.
1. Human teeth (adult), to show normal relationship of Hard Tissues.	1. Individual isolated Hard Tissues, *e.g.*, enamel prisms, dentine affected by caries etc., sheaths of Neumann, etc.
2. Jaws of animals, *e.g.*, rat, monkey, etc.	2. Alveolus and bone of jaw.
3. Teeth of large animals, horse elephant, etc.	3. Jaws with temporary and permanent teeth, *in situ*.
4. Fossil teeth.	4. The teeth of fish, pike, hake, etc
5. Certain pathological conditions of the Hard Tissues, *e.g.*, caries of dentine, exostosis of cementum, etc.	5. The teeth and jaws of small animals.
6. Cases in which it is necessary to retain the enamel.	6. Cases in which it is unnecessary to retain the enamel.
7. In connection with Weil's process.	7. In connection with the author's process.

CHAPTER III.

ON THE PREPARATION OF THE SOFT TISSUES.

To Prevent Shrinkage, etc.

THE difficulties attendant on the preparation of the soft dental tissues, for microscopic purposes, differ considerably from those discussed in the last chapter, and are of quite another nature. Here the great aim is to treat soft and delicate organs in such a manner that their individual cells, fibres, and other important elements, shall undergo no appreciable change in shape or appearance, either by shrinkage, swelling, or *post mortem* disintegration. It is obvious, therefore, that, in the first place, the tissues themselves must be perfectly fresh, and that the action of reagents on them must commence immediately after removal from their living condition: it is also clear that the simpler the method of preparation, the better the results: the shorter the time spent on preliminaries, *cæteris paribus*, the truer, and more faithful to nature will be the specimens under the microscope. It would be impossible, with a razor or knife, to satisfactorily cut a piece of soft tissue, the parts of which had not previously been treated and properly prepared; the friable cells and fibres, would, in that case, be broken up and hopelessly destroyed by the movements of the cutter alone. Hence, various reagents have to be employed.

The first steps are concerned with the performance of what are known as the processes of fixing and hardening the tissues. These generally occur simultaneously, but sometimes it is necessary first to fix, and afterwards to harden the specimen. This is done (*e.g.*, in Weil's method,) where mercury perchloride is used for fixing the soft parts, and alcohol for hardening them.

Reagents and their **Uses.**

Fixing the Tissues.—This means the coagulation of the albumenoids and gelatins of a living tissue, which occurs when it is brought into contact with a certain solution. The coagulating action fixes the delicate elements in the same position that they occupied during life. Many reagents may be used for this purpose, but of these the most useful for dental sections are, mercury, osmic acid, and copper. The first mentioned may be used either as a cold concentrated alcoholic solution of the perchloride, or a 5 per cent. aqueous solution: osmic acid—a 1 per cent. aqueous solution: and third, a saturated aqueous solution of acetate of copper. Alcohol in varying strengths is also an extremely valuable fixing agent. For mere fixing purposes, mercury is the best, although it leaves behind a troublesome precipitate, which requires removal by iodine. The disadvantages of employing osmic acid are, that it does not penetrate well (because only the external portion of the tissue is affected), that it stains, fixes, and hardens simultaneously, and that the operations have to be conducted in the dark. *Fixing.*

Whatever agent has been used, it is most important to remove it thoroughly from the tissues by immersion in alcohol, after complete fixation has taken place.

The "*Hardening*" of a piece of tissue has for its object the prevention of swelling or other changes in cells when placed in water or the staining *Hardening.*

solutions; and it gives such great consistency to specimens, that the thinnest possible sections can be cut, and be easily and safely manipulated.

The chief "hardening" reagents are, Müller's fluid, alcohol, picric acid, and picric with sulphuric acid when made up according to Fol's formula. Chromic acid, too, is sometimes used, alone or combined with osmic acid. Dr. Weil, of Munich, in his "Histologie der Zahn Pulpa," recommends as a useful fluid—a 1 per cent. solution of chromic acid, 100 c.c., with osmic acid (2 per cent. solution), 24 c.c., to which are added, afterwards, 6 c.c. of iced vinegar. "The tissue is then ready in a week." Dr. Sudduth considers that chromic acid alone is best. He uses a 1 per cent. solution, made by adding 30 grains of chromic acid to a quart of water. ("Dental Cosmos," 1884.)

Weil's Hardening Fluid.

Sudduth's System.

Of all these, the most useful and satisfactory for ordinary dental purposes are Müller's fluid, and alcohol, the former being especially suited for soft developmental tissues, as well as other structures, the latter for fully-grown specimens.

Müller's Fluid consists of potassium bichromate 2 parts, sodium sulphate 1 part, and distilled water 100 parts. The salts are generally sold mixed together as a reddish crystalline powder in bottles, and instructions are given for making the solution. If the student, however, wishes to make the solution himself, this can be done by mixing together and thoroughly incorporating, 3½ drachms of potassium bichromate, and 1½ drachms of sodium sulphate, and placing in a jar containing 1 pint of distilled water. Many advantages may be claimed for this reagent: it possesses great penetrating power, does not cause shrinkage of the cells, or fibrous tissues, and hardens uniformly. Sections are easy to manipulate, and are,

Müller's Fluid.

Its Composition.

Advantages.

as a rule, not brittle. Its sole disadvantage is that it slowly tinges the specimen a yellow colour, but this is invisible in microscopic sections and does not interfere with the staining. Its use is imperative if it is the student's intention to adopt for his sections Weigert's, Marchi's, Golgi's, or other special methods of staining. Müller's fluid may be sometimes usefully combined with methylated spirit, in the proportion of 3 of fluid to 1 of spirit. Specimens to be hardened must be cut into small pieces and placed in the fluid, which should be contained in large well-stoppered bottles or jars, after they have been washed for a few minutes in normal salt solution (common salt ·75 parts, and water 100 parts). The washing rids them of blood and other extraneous matters. About 20 times the bulk of Müller's fluid must be employed for each specimen. It must be changed on the second and fourth days, and then at the end of every week, the bottle or jar, meanwhile, being kept in a cool place. After a fortnight or three weeks have elapsed, the tissue is transferred to a bottle containing methylated spirit or rectified spirits of wine, in order that the hardening process may be completed, and the colouring matter removed.* *And Methods of Using.*

Alcohol, in the form of methylated spirit or rectified spirits of wine, will be found of great service in dental microscopy for the hardening of structures and organs less delicate than embryos. It is particularly of use in many pathological cases. It does not stain the specimen, and hardens more rapidly than the bichromates. It causes a certain amount of shrinkage, and must not be used if blood corpuscles are to be retained in the capillaries of a *Uses of Alcohol.*

---

* Some histologists prefer Erlicki's solution to Müller's fluid. Its constituents are the same as the latter, except that sulphate of copper is substituted for soda. It hardens a little more rapidly than Müller, but seems to possess no additional merit.

part. The quantity of spirit should exceed the bulk of the specimen by about ten times, and need not be changed until it becomes a little cloudy.

The ordinary methylated spirit contains mineral naphtha, and becomes turbid when mixed with water, (Squire, "Methods and Formulæ," 1892, p. 3). This form must, of course, be avoided, for valuable specimens may easily be ruined by it. The best methylated spirit, free from naphtha, may be obtained from wholesale houses.

Other "hardening" reagents might be mentioned, but the above are all that are requisite for dental microscopy.

Histological Classification of Soft Tissues.

The soft dental tissues may be conveniently classified as—

(i.) Developmental, including those found in the early or late ante-eruptive periods; and

(ii.) Completed or post-eruptive.

For both these groups of tissues, methods similar to those already described, are to be followed; although modifications in imbedding and staining may be introduced, the general principles of fixing and hardening must be adhered to. Details as to cutting sections will be given later.

A.

To Obtain and Prepare Specimens of the Soft Developmental Tissues.

Treatment of Embryonic Specimens. Remove several embryos and fœtuses from the uterus of some animal, *viz.*, pig, cat, dog, rabbit, which has been killed with a dose of bi-cyanide of mercury administered by the mouth, or perhaps better, by bleeding from the common carotids and jugulars, after chloroform anæsthesia. Decapitate the embryos, and rapidly wash the head in plenty of warm normal salt solution to remove all traces of blood. This should be done while the animal remains warm. It will be noticed that the heads will show various stages of growth.

If practicable, with all the fœtal heads, pass a sharp scalpel into the temporo-mandibular articulation on each side, and cut right back. The lower jaw will then be removed *in toto*. Divide this in the middle line, and then with a razor subdivide it still further, vertically, into small portions.

Each of these pieces is then again to be washed in salt solution, and immersed in Müller's fluid, freshly made. *Hardening.*

The upper jaws may be treated in the same manner, care being taken not to cut away the base of the skull.

After hardening is completed and the jaws decolorised by a fortnight's immersion in constantly changed alcohol, the pieces are allowed to soak for an hour in distilled water; they must then be transferred to a solution of gum mucilage prepared according to the formula of the British Pharmacopœia. It is advisable to add to this medium a little pure carbolic acid—10 drops to 1 ounce of mucilage. Here the pieces of tissue may remain for a lengthy period without deterioration. (Plate III.) *Imbedding.*

For *very* early embryonic jaws, fixing and hardening with mercury and alcohol, and imbedding in celloidin are distinctly indicated. As the jaws are too soft and small to be disarticulated, vertical sections should be made through the entire head.

The above remarks apply only to the earlier stages of developmental life, embryonic pigs, from one to six inches long being the most suitable animals to obtain.

Foetal Specimens.

Jaws of animals *at birth* may be treated as above, with the addition of the following precautions:—The tissues covering the mandible, lips, cheeks, &c., must be carefully stripped off, leaving nothing save the oral epithelium and flange of gum. Great care must be exercised not to use undue pressure on the soft parts; it is important that the scissors and scalpel should be very sharp. Best results can be obtained from vertical sections of the canine and bicuspid regions, because here the cap of dentine and enamel which is being formed, is very thin and but semi-calcified, and the movement of the microtome cutter or razor does not disturb the normal relations of the parts.

The jaws of kittens, rabbits, or pups at birth are most useful for this purpose.

B.

Hardening.

The Second Group of Tissues—including gum, pulp, periosteum, &c., may be treated as above, or with alcohol. If the latter is used, the specimens must be placed successively in 30, 50 and 70 per cent. spirit in watch-glasses, with twenty-four hours' immersion for each. They can then be kept in rectified spirits (84 per cent.) until required for imbedding and cutting.

Other Methods.

Campion's Method.

Mr. *G. G. Campion* uses chiefly perchloride of mercury and spirit as a fixing and hardening reagent for the preparation of specimens of pulp.

In a communication to the author he describes his method as follows:—" Immediately after extraction, wrap the tooth in a duster or piece of rag, and crack it in the jaws of a strong vice so as to expose the pulp thoroughly, then drop it into a saturated aqueous solution of mercury bi-chloride. This *fixes* the tissue, killing the cells and other tissue elements, so that they are but little affected by other reagents to which they may afterwards be subjected. The time required for fixing, varies with the size of the pulp, and the completeness of its exposure to the fluid. The process is completed when the tissue has become thoroughly whitened: it may take from one to twelve hours. Use glass or wood instruments to manipulate specimens in the mercury solution, as iron or steel produces a precipitate which may injure the tissue. When fixed, it is necessary to remove the bi-chloride entirely from the tissue, and complete the hardening by successive strengths of alcohol. Both these processes can be carried on at the same time by dropping the tooth, after removal from the bi-chloride solution, first into a tube filled with 30 per cent. alcohol to which a couple of drops of iodine liniment (or four or five drops of tincture) has been added, and then into a tube, (Wolrab's bottle) containing 50 per cent. alcohol, in which three or four pea-sized lumps of iodide of potassium have been dissolved. Leave the specimen for twelve hours in each tube, and afterwards, for the same time, in successive tubes containing 70 per cent. 90 per cent., and absolute alcohol.

"The iodine in the second tube throws down the mercury in the tissue as a red iodide, which is readily dissolved by the potassium iodide and alcohol in the third tube. After remaining for twelve hours in absolute alcohol, the pulp must be carefully removed from the broken tooth with a scalpel, and placed in a tube or small dish containing cedar oil, on the surface of which a little absolute alcohol has been gently poured. These two fluids do not easily mix, and when the pulp has sunk to the bottom of the cedar oil it is ready for imbedding in paraffin, according to Mr. Mummery's method. The above is a modification of the method of hardening used in the Weil process."

Marson's Method.

Mr. *Cyril Marson*, in the "Journal of the British Dental Association," Vol. xiv., No. 7, recommends the following:—"A large bottleful of a solution of chromic acid in water of a strength of one-sixth per cent. must be made. For two or three specimens, two wineglassfuls of this, and one of methylated spirit must be mixed in a bottle or jar. The specimens are left in this for twenty-four hours, and the bottle occasionally shaken; the liquid is now poured off and a fresh supply given. In this they must remain thirty-six hours; two more supplies of solution must be given, in each of which the specimens must remain forty-eight hours. After this, they may be transferred to methylated spirit and kept until required. During this process, the specimens ought to be kept in a cupboard or dark room. Should they contain any calcified teeth or bone, hydrochloric acid in the proportion of about five or six drops to the ounce, must be added to the two last hardening solutions before placing in the methylated spirit."

Rothmann's Method.

Dr. *Rothmann*,[*] of Buda Pesth, proceeds in the following manner, in the case of investigating diseases of the pulp and periosteum.

(*a*) Tooth is washed in distilled water, and placed in absolute alcohol.

(*b*) Periosteum is detached from cementum by a sharp gouge or chisel.

(*c*) Tooth is split with a chisel or forceps and pulp carefully removed in its entirety.

---

[*] "Patho Histologie der Zahnpulpa und Wurzelhaut," Stuttgart, 1889.

(*d*) Pulp is then stained, imbedded in celloidin, hardened in alcohol, cut on a microtome and mounted in balsam.

Demonstration of Special Soft Tissues.

The Absorbent Organ can be obtained after the removal of a loose temporary molar, by snipping off with fine pointed scissors the soft tissue observed on the summit of the permanent tooth beneath. This is washed in salt solution for a moment, and placed in Müller's fluid for a week, then in alcohol for a fortnight. It should be imbedded in celloidin or paraffin. *Absorbent Organ.*

The cells of the absorbent organ *in situ* are best demonstrated by treating a temporary tooth by Weil's method (Plate VI., Fig. 4). *Another Method.*

The blood supply of developing teeth can be shewn by the methods of injection of capillaries (*see* Chapter VII.); the jaws are then removed, hardened in Müller's fluid and alcohol, and imbedded in gum or celloidin (*see* Plate VII., Fig. 3). *Vascular Supply.*

To obtain specimens of the *Dental Follicle* and so-called "*Gubernaculum*." Purchase the lower jaw of a young heifer, which has just been killed, place it in a vice, and make vertical saw cuts between contiguous teeth in the incisor and canine regions: permanent teeth will be discovered enclosed in the follicle in the substance of the jaw. Cut slices from this soft tissue, wash, immerse in methylated spirit, and then transfer to rectified spirit for a month. Wash again and imbed in gum mucilage. *Dental Follicle.*

The Dental Gum can be sectionized after similar treatment to that just mentioned. It is better to prepare specimens *in situ* by the author's process. *Dental Gum.*

Dental Pulp, and its Chief Elements.

Methods for Obtaining Sections of the Dental Pulp.

(i.) Crack a tooth longitudinally in a vice or with excising forceps, or fracture it with a hammer, and gently remove the soft organ with a pair of fine forceps or a needle-point. Treat it with Müller's fluid or alcohol.

(ii.) Sections can be quickly made by immersing a removed pulp in a 1 per cent. solution of osmic acid, which hardens the tissue and stains the nerve bundles. The organ should remain in the acid for twenty-four hours in the dark, or until such time that delicate dark lines—stained nerve fasciculi—are visible on its surface. Then wash with distilled water, and transfer to 70 per cent. alcohol till convenient to soak in gum solution.

The pulp nerves may be teased out by means of needle points, and then mounted at once, in normal salt solution. For a method of holding the needles *see* Fig. 5.

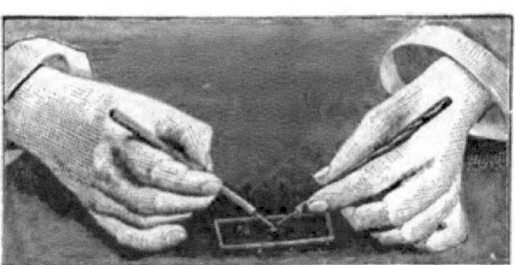

Fig. 5.
METHOD OF HOLDING THE NEEDLES
FOR TEASING OUT SPECIMENS.

If the structure of the medullated nerves is to be demonstrated, it is more convenient to use the incisor pulps of the ox.

(iii.) Pulp sections are always better when cut *in situ*, either by Weil's or the author's special process.

Isolated odontoblasts may be well studied by (i.) teasing them from the cap of dentine which is being produced in developmental specimens. A section having been cut on the microtome, is placed on a glass slide and its parts carefully separated by means of needle points. (ii.) Odontoblasts may also be obtained by splitting a tooth in a vice, removing the pulp, and scraping them, with the point of a sharp knife, from the surface of the pulp cavity, to which they closely adhere.

The mass so obtained should be laid on a slide, separated with needle-points, a drop of normal salt solution or glycerine jelly added, and a cover-glass applied and pressed down flat. They should be stained with solutions run under the cover-glass.

To demonstrate the long central processes of these cells, place an isolated dental pulp for 24 hours in a ·6 per cent. solution of potassium anhydrochromate, and tease out in picro-carmine small fragments of its periphery.*

Much information of an interesting nature concerning the morphology of the *odontoblasts when observed in situ*, may be gained by studying pulps of varying ages—

>(i.) They are seen in their most active state in vertical sections made through the canine region of the mandible of pup at birth.

>(ii.) In transverse sections of adult human teeth whose roots are only partially developed.

>(iii.) In transverse sections of adult canine teeth taken through the cervical region.

---

* Aitchison Robertson—Trans. Odonto-Chirurg. Soc., Nov., 1892.

Pulp Tissues. In the last mentioned instance, the marked difference in shape is noticed, if the odontoblasts situated at the periphery of the long diameter of the pulp be compared with those in the short diameter.

Prepare specimens of (i.) by hardening in Müller's fluid and alcohol, and cutting on a microtome; of (ii.) by Weil's process; of (iii.) by the author's process.

Table of Soft Tissues suitable for Preliminary Treatment with

MÜLLER'S FLUID AND ALCOHOL.	ALCOHOL. (84 per cent).	MERCURY PERCHLORIDE, AND ALCOHOL.
1. Jaws of fœtal animals.	1. Dental pulp, and peridental membrane.	1. Dental pulp, *in situ*, in young teeth, with incompleted roots.
2. Dental pulp, and certain of its pathological conditions.	2. Soft tissues in connection with large animals' jaws and teeth.	2. Isolated dental pulp.
3. Peridental membrane, and its pathological conditions.	3. Dental gum.	3. Peridental membrane.
4. In cases where special stainings are to be subsequently used.	4. Dental follicle when fully formed.	4. Cells of absorbent organ.
5. Absorbent organ isolated.		5. Very early embryonic jaws of animals.

CHAPTER IV.

ON THE PREPARATION OF THE HARD AND SOFT TISSUES COMBINED.

DENTAL histologists have of late years begun to recognise the importance of studying sections, where the soft parts are retained in their normal relationship to the harder tissues, with which they are so closely associated. Much time and labour have been spent in working out plans to attain this end; and, while considerable advancements have recently been made, one is still bound to admit, that, of all the processes known for this special purpose, not one satisfies the critic in every particular. This is easily understood when the remarkable density of bone, dentine, and cementum, and the extreme delicacy of structures, like the pulp or periosteum, are taken into account. Reagents applied for one purpose to a tissue, react often on other tissues, and imperfect results are obtained. *Retention of soft parts in situ.*

There are, however, three chief methods of preparing specimens, the details of which, if carefully followed, lead to results which are approximately correct: and as such, one must be content to adopt these plans until some newer and more perfect suggestions are put forth. These are known as the chromic acid process, Weil's balsam process, and Hopewell Smith's process.

The Chromic Acid Process.

This, the oldest process, is one in which chromic acid is used in the dual capacity of a hardening and *For developmental tissues.*

softening reagent. It is very slow in its action; but it serves the purpose well when the student desires to make sections of embryonic jaws, of developmental growths in which hard tissue is present, and of fully grown teeth *in situ*. Its details are as follow:—

The jaw—preferably the lower—of an animal, such as a cat, dog, or monkey, is removed while still fresh, and washed in normal salt solution. It is then subdivided into vertical pieces, and immersed in a solution containing—

Chromic acid	45 grains.
Nitric acid	1½ drachms.
Water	1 pint.

Simultaneous Softening and Hardening. The fluid should be kept in a stoppered jar or bottle, and renewed at the end of the second day, a large quantity being used for a small piece of tissue. The latter presents, after some time, a green appearance, due to the formation of chromic sesquioxide; but this colouring is invisible in microscopic sections.

When the tissue has become completely flexible and soft, removal and well washing for a lengthy period under a tap are indicated, and then immersion for one to two hours in a neutralising solution of bicarbonate of soda, 1 drachm to 1 pint of water. The object is again washed, and finally transferred to gum mucilage, whence it is taken for microtome cutting.

In this way, if double staining be used, very beautiful and instructive slides may be made of those developing teeth in which the cap of dentine is thick, and also of temporary and permanent teeth, *in situ*, to demonstrate the method of eruption. (Plate VI., Fig. 1) The enamel becomes, however, softened and removed *in toto*.

Dr. Weil, of Munich, has elaborated a plan in which the main feature is impregnation by balsam, after special preparation, followed later by grinding on a stone. The details were published * in England in 1888, and Mr. J. Howard Mummery introduced this process to the Odontological Society of Great Britain in 1890. The process attains very nearly to perfection; and if it is carried out in minute detail, highly satisfactory results are attained. Nevertheless it is open to several objections, amongst which, may be noticed, its tediousness and length of performance which requires constant attention, its inadaptibility to numerous important nuclear and specific stains, and its prolonged treatment with many and varied reagents at different degrees of temperature. *Weil's Method.* *Advantages.* *Disadvantages.*

Weil's Process.

(i.) Freshly extracted teeth are divided into several pieces with a sharp, fine fret-saw (watch spring saw), by being held between the fingers under cold water trickling from a tap, or squeezed from a clean sponge. This division enables reagents and stains to penetrate quickly and evenly into the pulp. *Modus Operandi.*

(ii.) The pieces are then laid in a concentrated aqueous solution of corrosive sublimate for some hours, 6 or 8 being necessary as a rule. The mercury "fixes" the soft tissues, through coagulation of their albumens and gelatins. *Fixing.*

(iii.) They are then placed in a dish, and water from a tap is allowed to wash them well for one hour.

(iv.) Removal to 30 per cent. alcohol is the next step. Here they remain for twelve hours. After transference to 50 per cent. and 70 per cent. alcohol for corresponding periods of time, they are put into a bottle containing 90 per cent. alcohol, to which has been added 1·5 or 2 per cent. of tincture of iodine.

---

* "Journal Royal Microscopical Society, 1888," p. 1042.

Removal of Mercury.   The iodine removes the precipitate in the tissue, by the production of iodide of mercury, which in its turn is eliminated from the specimen by a prolonged immersion in absolute alcohol. The teeth then appear quite white.

Staining.   (v.) Again the pieces of teeth are well washed under the tap, and stains are now used, Weil recommending borax-carmine. Grenacher's is the best for staining in bulk; but the alcoholic and not the aqueous must be used, as it penetrates well, and does not gelatinize, which the latter is apt to do after a time. Mr. Mummery has found that aniline blue-black stains efficiently in this process, and that it is particularly useful for ulterior photo-micrographic purposes. Immersion in the colouring solution is prolonged. The time varies as to the thickness of the pieces, but from three to seven days will generally suffice.

(vi.) In order to fix the stain, it is necessary next to pass the pieces into acidulated alcohol, *viz.*, 100 c.m. of 70 per cent. alcohol, to which 1 c.m. of hydrochloric or acetic acid has been added. Here they remain for twenty-four or thirty-six hours. If an aqueous stain has been used, half that time will be sufficient.

(vii.) The pieces are now transferred to 90 per cent. alcohol for fifteen minutes, and afterwards to absolute alcohol for half an hour. This prepares them for clearing.

Clearing.   (viii.) Oil of cloves or oil of cedar wood is to be used, and pieces remain here for twelve hours.

(ix.) The oil is next quickly washed off with xylol, and the pieces suspended in pure chloroform.

Balsam Impregnation.   (x.) Twenty-four hours later they are saturated in a chloroform extract of dried or desiccated Canada balsam, made about the consistency of treacle. They should be kept in this chloroform balsam for a day, and then more dried balsam is added to the solution until the chloroform can no longer take it up. Only a little is to be added at a time. This stage is reached in three or four days.

(xi.) The prepared pieces are finally placed in a china jar or other receptacle over a water bath kept at the temperature of 90° C. or 194° F. They remain here for two or three days or more, until the balsam in which they are imbedded, when quite cooled, cracks like glass on the introduction of a needle point into it.

(xii.) Thin sections are now made, by again cutting each piece into halves with a fret-saw under water, each piece being then ground down on a corundum or carborundum wheel on the lathe, and lastly rubbed on a Washita stone with the finger. Chloroform balsam is to be used as the mountant. *Grinding.*

Mr. Mummery recommends Wolrab's gold cylinder bottles, labelled, as being most convenient for holding the various reagents through which specimens have to pass during the stages of the process. If a note of the stage they have reached be made on the labels of the different bottles, and the stages begun at different times, the process is not so complicated or troublesome as might at first be imagined. With reference to the process itself, special care should be taken in keeping the specimens sufficiently long over the water bath, because if this is not done, when the student begins to grind down the pieces, portions of the pulp, if not the whole organ, will be dragged away. On the other hand, prolonged heating leads to brittleness, the temperature should therefore never exceed 90° C. Rapid grinding should not be attempted; a slow cutting stone gives best results, and does not fill *Precautions.*

the tissue with detritus. The preparations seem to grind down more easily if they are left for some weeks exposed to the air previous to cutting on the wheel. The use of an indiarubber finger-stall has been found by Mr. Sydney Spokes to be extremely satisfactory in finishing the rubbing down of tolerably thin sections, during the final stages of Weil's process. The indiarubber seems to "surround" the specimen better, and hold it more firmly than do the finger-tips. It also prevents the latter from coming into contact with the stone.

Spoke's Methods of Finishing.

In cases where trouble may be threatened by the different rate of wear when grinding hard and soft dental tissues, such as sections of jaw with temporary or permanent teeth *in situ*, the same worker adopts the following ingenious precaution:— One side of a somewhat thick specimen is ground smooth, and it is then sunk, finished side downwards, into a piece of softened A 1 composition, the other surface of the composition being pinched up to make a kind of "handle." The surface of the section to be still further ground, is turned on to a glass slab, whilst the composition becomes cold. Both slab and section should be first well wetted, so that the composition does not adhere to them. One is thus enabled to make a matrix filling the irregular outline of the section, in which the latter may be conveniently ground until very thin.

The Use of a Matrix.

Hopewell Smith's Process.

This method, like the preceding, has for its object the retention, *in situ*, of the hard and soft tissues. It was brought before the Odontological Society of Great Britain, in November, 1891, and a complete account of it can be found in that society's transactions. Its advantages are, briefly:—

Advantages.

the retention of the soft parts in close juxtaposition to the hard tissues (*viz.*, pulp to dentine, peridental membrane to cementum or bone), the great ease and rapidity of its performance, its extreme simplicity, its adaptability to any method of imbedding in gum, celloidin, or paraffin, thus allowing, if desired, serial sections to be made. In addition, any number of sections can be cut in any direction from the same tooth, and by using a microtome these sections can be made thinner than by grinding down methods. There is a quick and permanent penetration of stains, which may be of any kind. Its great disadvantage is that the enamel is not preserved, as the acids rapidly soften and remove this tissue entirely. It is certain, too, that the hard tissues are chemically changed during the removal of their lime salts, but no appreciable alteration in structure can be noticed, this compensating in a great degree for the chemical differences that have occurred. M. Choquet,* of the École Dentaire de Paris, speaks in praise of the acid solution and this process, but thinks that it has "a dissolving action on the nuclei of the cells (of the soft parts)." He suggests the addition of a 1 per cent. solution of chloride of palladium to obviate this "inconvenience." *Disadvantages.*

Details of the Process.—A newly-extracted tooth is well washed in normal salt solution for some minutes. In order to allow reagents to penetrate into the pulp, it is often necessary to enlarge the apical foramen or foramina with a fissure bur on the dental engine, and to make a counter opening through the crown. As a rule it is better to divide the tooth into halves, by cutting through the cervical region with a sharp fret-saw, allowing *Preliminary. Treatment.*

---

* "Traité Technique des Préparations Microscopiques," 1895, p. 80.

meanwhile a good supply of salt solution to moisten the dentine. In those cases where the pulp chamber is opened, by the progress of caries, these precautions need not be taken.

Hardening. The pieces are now placed in a stoppered jar containing freshly-made Müller's fluid, the volume of the latter being about twenty to thirty times the bulk of the tooth. Fresh fluid should be used on the fourth day, and this changed again at the end of a fortnight. At the end of three weeks, pieces should be removed to alcohol (84 per cent.) for ten to twenty days or more. Rectified spirits of wine may be used in place of Müller's fluid from the first, and is preferable in some cases. Thus the delicate soft tissues are fixed and hardened. The portions of tooth are now taken from the

Protection of Soft Parts. hardening fluid and well washed. The soft parts and the apices of the roots must be dried on a cloth, and a large drop of flexile collodion or celloidin placed on them, in such a manner that in a few moments a thick film covers them over, and will protect them from the action of the acid

Decalcifying. reagents. The tooth is now placed in 12 c.c. of a 10 per cent. solution of hydrochloric acid, freshly made. A Wolrab's bottle is very useful for holding this decalcifying fluid. It should be labelled, and the hour of immersion and character of the specimen noted. At the end of fifteen hours, add 1·5 c.c. of strong, pure (non-fuming) nitric acid to the hydrochloric acid solution, and repeat this at the end of forty-eight hours. In about three or three-and-a-half days (seventy to eighty hours) the whole of the dentine and cementum should be completely decalcified. Temporary teeth and molars will require a shorter or longer acid immersion. The student must of course be guided by the amount of softening that has already taken place. This can be easily ascertained by trying to bend the specimen with the fingers or piercing it with a needle point.

If sufficiently decalcified, the tooth must be washed and placed in a solution of bicarbonate of soda or lithium (5 grains to the ounce) for half-an-hour, after which it is to be further subdivided by a sharp scalpel or razor, and the pieces well washed and put into gum mucilage solution. Here *Saturating.* they remain for at least fifteen hours, care being taken that the pieces of tissue are not cut too large for complete saturation by gum. Removal of the film of collodion is best effected by allowing the tooth to remain in a watch glass of ether for about five minutes, and carefully picking or rubbing it off with a brush. This should be done before it is passed into the neutralising solution. The pieces of tissue are finally placed on the stage of an ether freezing microtome and cut in the ordinary manner. *Cutting Sections.* For the gum solution there may be substituted celloidin or paraffin—the former must be used if the tissues are exceedingly delicate and friable, and the latter, if serial sections are required.

Sections having been made, are next washed, stained, and mounted in the usual way.

Special Points.—The hard parts must not be too *Precautions.* much decalcified, the collodion film must cover up all the soft tissues, and the specimens must remain for a sufficient length of time in the gum solution. If the latter has been used as a saturating agent, it is advisable occasionally to dehydrate sections in the following manner:—

They should be transferred from a watch glass *Special Dehydration.* containing 30 per cent. spirit, to 70 and 90 per cent., and absolute alcohol. The period of immersion in the varying strengths of alcohol should be one minute. This is to prevent the delicate pulp tissue from shrinking from the softened dentine walls, which sometimes occurs if the sections are at once placed in absolute alcohol.

D. Caush's Method.

Mr. D. E. Caush, in the "Journal of the British Dental Association," suggests "A simple method of staining and cutting hard and soft sections combined." He writes:—

"Take a freshly extracted tooth, and if it has a live pulp, place in alcohol for twenty-four hours to harden the pulp. On taking the tooth out of the alcohol, place it in a stain 'made by dissolving any of the usual dyes in alcohol', for two or three days. On removing the tooth from the dye, grind on the flat side of a corundum wheel, until the pulp is *almost* exposed; afterwards grind the opposite side until you have a section of the tooth, with a slight covering of hard tissue on either side of the pulp. Now finish grinding down between two pieces of ground glass, with a small quantity of pumice powder moistened with alcohol or methylated spirit, until the section is as thin as required; towards the end of the grinding, use plenty of the liquid with little or no pumice powder. When ground down, wash thoroughly in distilled water; dry off the *surface moisture*, and mount in Canada balsam. With ordinary care, sections may be made with the hard and soft tissues in position. If we want to show the tubuli of the dentine, or bloodvessels, lacunæ, &c., of alveolus, place at once in the stain, and in the case of a tooth, the stain will pass up the pulp canal, and permeate the dentine by passing through the tubuli; after the tooth has remained in the stain for a day or two, prepare as above. Sections so prepared are especially adapted for examination with $\frac{1}{4}$ or $\frac{1}{8}$ inch objective."

The method seems to answer very well for making specimens of alveolar bone with the soft tissues retained *in situ*, but it is not conducive to best results to place the tooth in alcohol as directed, until an opening has first been made into the pulp chamber, so that the spirit can easily reach the soft tissues. *For what Available.*

*Summary of Weil's Process.**

Fresh teeth cut under water with watch spring saw. *Summary.*

Concentrated corrosive sublimate solution for some hours.

Running water, one hour or more.

30 per cent. spirit, twelve hours.

50 per cent. spirit, twelve hours.

70 per cent. spirit, twelve hours.

90 per cent. spirit and 2 per cent. iodine, twelve hours.

Absolute alcohol till teeth are white.

Running water, half-an-hour.

Stain, borax carmine, etc., three to seven days, according to stain used.

70 per cent. spirit (and 1 per cent HCl if borax carmine), twelve to thirty-six hours.

90 per cent spirit, fifteen minutes.

Absolute alcohol, half an hour.

Etherial oil, twelve hours.

Wash this off with xylol.

Chloroform, twenty-four hours.

Thin solution of dried Canada balsam in chloroform.

---

* See, for this and the following summary, "Transactions Odontological Society," Vol. XXII., p. 222, and Vol. XXIV., p. 20.

Thick solution of dried Canada balsam in chloroform.

Water bath at 90° C. till hard.

Summary of Author's Process.

Summary. Immerse a newly extracted tooth, after division with a fret-saw, under salt solution, in Müller's fluid for three to four weeks, and remove to spir. vini. rect. for ten to twenty days. Alcohol (84 per cent.) may be used instead of Müller's fluid.

Remove, wash in water, and seal up apical foramen and soft parts with collodion.

Place tooth in 15 c.c. of following solution:—

HCl, 12 parts (pure).
HNO_3, 30 parts (non-fuming).
Aq. dest., 108 parts.

Thus:—Take 12 c.c. of 10 per cent. solution of HCl, and at end of fifteen hours add 1·5 c.c. of HNO_3 and and at end of forty-eight hours add 1·5 c.c. of HNO_3 from commencement of immersion in acid solution.

Remove tooth at end of seventy-five to eighty hours or more and wash in a solution of lithium carb. (5 grains to an ounce) for half-an-hour. Wash thoroughly with distilled water.

Divide tooth by razor into several pieces and wash again in water. Place each in gum mucilage (B.P.). Leave in mucilage twelve to fifteen hours or more.

Transfer to stage of freezing microtome, cut, wash sections, and stain with orange-rubine, or gold chloride, or borax-carmine, or Weigert's solutions.

Dehydrate in absolute alcohol three minutes, "clear" in cedar oil one and a-half minutes, and mount in Canada balsam.

Table of Tissues suitable for Preparation by

Chromic Acid Process.	Weil's Process.	Author's Process.
1. Jaws of human and comparative embryos which contain large areas of hard tissues.	1. Pulp *in situ*.	1. Pulp *in situ* in both temporary and permanent teeth.
	2. Pulp in connection with semi-calcified dentine.	2. Peridental membrane *in situ*
2. Jaws of animals with temporary and permanent teeth *in situ*.	3. Calcification of dentine.	3. Dental gum *in situ*.
	4. Teeth with incompleted roots.	4. Teeth of fish and animals where soft tissues are to be preserved.
3. Fully developed human teeth.	5. Adult teeth *in situ*.	5. In all pathological conditions, except affections of the enamel.
	6. Peridental membrane *in situ*.	
	7. Absorbent organ *in situ*.	
	8. Absorption occurring in adult teeth.	

CHAPTER V.

ON IMBEDDING AND CUTTING SECTIONS.

THE chief modes of preparing the various dental tissues for histological examination having already been described, it is now necessary to consider the means at the disposal of the student, whereby all soft and softened tissues may be imbedded and cut. The object of the preliminary treatment of specimens by fixing, hardening, and decalcifying reagents, has been to render them fit for imbedding, prior to cutting them into sections on a microtome.

Object of Imbedding. When a piece of tissue is imbedded, it is placed in a suitable medium of proper consistency, which is intended to run into and fill all the interstices, not only saturating and impregnating it throughout, but holding its delicate structures in position until a razor or cutter divides it into the thinnest possible sections.

General Principles.

There are two methods of imbedding—(i.) simple, and (ii.) interstitial.

In the former, tissues are simply fixed in another medium, and mechanically retained until cut. It is useless for dental work, and need not be further considered here.

Interstitial imbedding implies that the substance penetrates into, and is retained within the tissue; and there are three important media for achieving this purpose—gum mucilage, celloidin, and paraffin. Their nature, advantages, functions, and methods of using must now be detailed in particular.

The Employment of Gum Mucilage.

The British Pharmacopœial form of gum solution is most convenient. It can be bought already made, or obtained by dissolving four ounces of "picked" gum acacia in six ounces of water. If carbolic acid, in the proportion of ten drops of a saturated solution to the ounce, is added, tissues prepared for cutting can be kept in the mass all the year round, without undergoing deterioration, loss of water by evaporation being occasionally renewed. A combination of five parts of syrup (one pound of lump sugar to one pint of boiling water) to three parts of mucilage is said to make the impregnation more complete. *Gum Mucilage.*

Of all imbedding media, gum mucilage is found to be the most useful for ordinary dental microscopical work; it is suitable for nearly every class of tissue. Its merits are many. The preliminary steps — such as it is necessary to perform when specimens are about to be imbedded in celloidin or paraffin—are reduced to a minimum, much time and labour are saved, and the procedure is simple, rapid, and clean. Small pieces of tissue having been soaked in water for some hours to remove all traces of the "preparation" reagents, are placed in a large quantity of mucilage. Here they should remain from ten to fifteen hours or more, according to the size of the tissue. The criterion for complete saturation is afforded by the fact that the specimen falls to the bottom of the bottle or jar when it *Advantages.*

Method of Using.

cannot take up any more of the medium. It is then in a fit state to be frozen and cut into sections.

Microtome. The student, at this point of his work, should obtain the use of an ether freezing microtome. There are several useful varieties; but the beginner cannot do better than use a Cathcart's microtome. It may be said that with this, as with other instruments, practice only will lead to satisfactory results. When once the knack is attained, section cutting becomes a simple and easy matter.

Fig. 6.

CATHCART'S MICROTOME, SHOWING THE METHOD OF USING THE CUTTER, AND THE WAY IN WHICH SECTIONS ARE MADE.

Cathcart's Microtome.

The accompanying figure exhibits the chief points of Cathcart's instrument. It will be seen that the tissue is raised by means of a large differential screw beneath, and that the cutter moves from behind forwards and is not automatic.

Method of Using.—The microtome is clamped to the edge of a firm table, and the bottle half-filled with ether. Ether sulph. meth. sp. gr. ·735, or ether rect. opt. (Etheris Purus B.P.), sp. gr. ·720, answers equally well for freezing purposes. A slice of the specimen, not more than ⅛ inch thick, is now placed in the middle of the plate, and a drop or two of gum mucilage allowed to fall on the top and run down its sides equally in all directions. An assistant should manipulate the bellows, and direct a continuous spray of ether on the under surface of the stage. It may be necessary to add more gum, until at length the object is frozen right through in a solid mass. The plane must be held firmly with the right hand, and rapidly pushed through the specimen, while the left hand slightly moves the milled head at every stroke of the cutter. The sections should collect in a little heap on the upper surface of the plane; if they fly off, or curl up, the tissue is too much frozen, and the assistant must cease using the bellows for a moment, the operator meanwhile breathing gently on the object. The sections should then be carefully removed from the plane by a small wet camel's hair brush, and be dropped into a black vulcanite tray—a photographic quarter-plate developing dish filled with water makes an excellent receiver. Here they will separate of their own accord, in a few minutes. The whole or part of the prepared tissue having been thus sectionised, a piece of ordinary glass is placed over the vulcanite dish to protect the floating sections from dust. They may then be examined at leisure, and the thinnest, *i.e.*, the most transparent, chosen, and placed in a bottle containing 30 or 50 per cent. alcohol until the student has time to stain and mount them.

To Cut Sections.

To Cut Sections.

The cutter should be set and stropped before each time of using, and at the end of the operation washed with alcohol, and wiped on a rag which has been smeared with vaseline. The microtome also should be wiped dry, and kept in a box to protect it.

The apparatus can be obtained from Baker, of High Holborn.

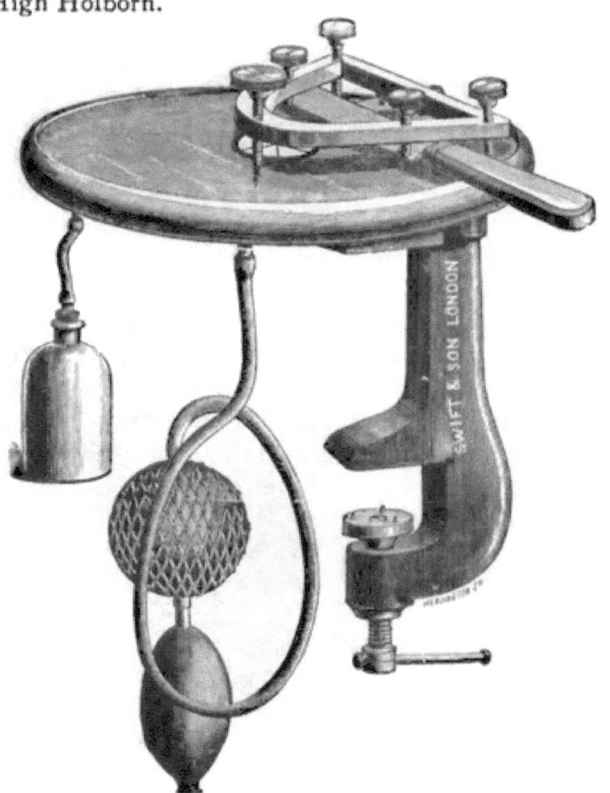

Fig. 7.

SWIFT'S ETHER-FREEZING MICROTOME.

A larger and more useful form of apparatus is shown above. This is Swift's modification of Williams' microtome. Here, the cutter, similar in size and shape to a razor, is fastened into a frame,

CUTTING SECTIONS. 57

provided with three delicate screws, which regulate the thinness of the sections. The movements are in an opposite direction to those of Cathcart's knife, *viz.*, towards the operator, who has thus greater control over the cutter. The tissue is firmly fixed, and cannot be heightened or lowered.

Method of Using. Before using this instrument, moisten its upper glass surface with a little water; this makes the cutter frame run quite smoothly. Place the tissue on the stage and freeze as before directed. Hold the frame very firmly with the fingers of both hands, the thumbs being towards the operator; and by means of the right thumb move the anterior screw through a quarter of a revolution or less at each stroke. This requires practice.

How to Hold the Frame.

The sections collect on the knife, and are placed in a tray of water as already described.

The chief feature of Roy's Freezing Microtome, which is the best and most convenient ether-freezing apparatus made, is that it is automatic. It can also be used for cutting specimens imbedded in celloidin, the slicing movement of the razor being well adapted for this purpose.

Advantages of Roy's Instrument.

Fig. 8.

ROY'S IMPROVED FREEZING MICROTOME.

Roy's Microtome.

Method of Using.—The razor should be clamped quite near its end, as shown in the cut, and raised to its highest position above the plate. This is done by moving the horizontal brass handle to and fro, the ratchet click engaging with the teeth of the ratchet wheel on the further side of the instrument. The reverse of this will lower the razor, and razor holder. Sections are made by moving the wooden handle backwards and forwards, their thickness depending on the distance that the brass handle is moved at each stroke.

The microtome is made by the Cambridge Scientific Company, and can be highly recommended.

Imbedding in Celloidin.

The employment of celloidin as an imbedding medium for dental tissues, has not received the support of histologists that it deserves. It is an extremely useful agent. It possesses, at once, not only great penetrative power, and equal uniformity of permeation, but is remarkable for the ease with which it can be manipulated.

One finds it most invaluable for imbedding frail delicate organs, whose parts are but loosely held together; such as early embryonic jaws and teeth, decalcified fish's teeth, decalcified teeth with pulps *in situ*, etc.

Celloidin is a preparation of pure pyroxylin, and is merely a patented collodion. Schering's celloidin is the best. It is obtained in the form of thick plates of a tough, gelatinous, semi-transparent substance, which should be cut up into shavings before using.

Steps of the Process.

Modus Operandi.

(A) *Infiltration.* Have ready four glass-stoppered bottles, labelled, and containing (i.) ABSOLUTE

ALCOHOL, (ii.) ALCOHOL AND ETHER, (iii.) THIN CELLOIDIN, and (iv.) THICK CELLOIDIN. For the second bottle make a mixture of equal parts of absolute alcohol and methylated ether. It is difficult to give the exact proportions of the celloidin solutions; they are both made by adding the shavings of celloidin to varying quantities of alcohol and ether. The "thick" solution should be of a thick syrupy consistence, the "thin" being the same diluted with absolute alcohol and ether. The object of using these two solutions is to make certain of getting a complete impregnation of the tissues.

The object having been dehydrated by immersion in absolute alcohol for twenty-four hours, is placed in the second mixture for the same period. It should then be removed and suspended in the thin celloidin, and finally in the thick solution, remaining in each, from one day to one week. The length of time depends on the size of the object.

(*B*) *Imbedding.* After thorough infiltration, the tissue is imbedded. Twist a piece of stout writing paper round a small cork, in such a manner that it projects from one end, and makes a collar. Stick a pin through the paper into the cork, and paint the line of junction with celloidin solution. After this is set, fill the paper thimble with thick solution, and suspend the object in the middle of it. Expose it to the air to dry. In a few minutes, a film will form over the surface of the celloidin, and then the paper thimble, with its contents, should be placed in a jar of pure chloroform,* free from water. Here, in one or two days, the celloidin will be thoroughly hardened.

Paper Cell for Imbedding

---

* Many workers use methylated spirit and water instead of chloroform to harden the celloidin block.

Next remove the imbedded object from the chloroform, and tear off its paper support, leaving a clear block of celloidin. Then either place the block in a vial of white oil of thyme, as suggested by Bumpus,* to clear it, or put it at once into the clamp of a microtome. Use for this purpose the clamp supplied with Roy's freezing microtome. (*See* Fig. 8.) Keep the razor well moistened with spirit or oil of thyme, and take off the sections with a camel's hair brush.

Staining. It is better, in the majority of cases, to stain the tissue *en masse*, before imbedding, using borax or lithium carmine (Grenacher's). But some workers † prefer to stain the sections after cutting. The writer, however, considers the other method the better. In any case, sections must be dehydrated again in absolute alcohol, and cleared in cedar-wood oil or xylol, and *not* oil of cloves. They are to be mounted subsequently in Canada balsam.

Alternative Plan. Celloidin imbedded specimens may be cut into sections by freezing on an ordinary Cathcart's microtome, provided they have been hardened in alcohol. The block should be kept in running water for at least one day to remove the alcohol, and then transferred to gum mucilage, and cut after some hours.

Much better sections, however, can be obtained by using Roy's instrument, because of the mowing movements of the razor.

Serial Section Imbedding and Cutting.

If the student intends to do research work, he will find it often desirable to make sections of an organ in series. In dental microscopy this applies

---

* "Amer. Natur.," Vol. XXVI, 1892, pp. 80, 81.
† Stirling's "Practical Histology," 1893, p. 45.

chiefly to developmental tissues, and pathological conditions of the pulp, or peridental membrane. From what has been already said, it will be at once seen that it is a difficult thing to do serial section cutting, if gum or celloidin are used as imbedding media. Paraffin and a special form of microtome have therefore to be employed.

Imbedding in Paraffin.

Mr. Howard Mummery advocates the following methods of dehydration and imbedding :— *Mummery's Method of Imbedding.*

After the tissue has been fixed and hardened, it is put into 50 per cent. alcohol for two hours, then into 70 per cent. for twenty-four hours, followed by 80 per cent. for twelve hours, and 95 per cent. for two hours, complete dehydration being finally produced by a short immersion in absolute alcohol. Wolrab's bottles, well corked, are very useful for this dehydration process.

"Clearing" is the next step, and cedar-wood oil or turpentine are to be used. Pour some of the medium into a test tube, and on the top put a little absolute alcohol. Carefully place the object in the alcohol, and allow it to sink to the bottom of the test tube, afterwards drawing off the alcohol with a pipette.

The clarifying oil has prepared it for the imbedding medium, which is hard paraffin. A lump of paraffin should be placed in a water-bath, and kept at a temperature of 45° C.—its melting point. The object is placed therein, and it should remain there for one or two days. The paraffin at the end of that time is allowed to cool, and when it becomes hard it can be cut out of the water-bath dish or tray.

The block is fixed on to the object carrier of a Rocking Microtome by melting with a hot knife the *Fixing the Block.*

Cutting Serial Sections. surface of the block and the paraffin already attached to the carrier. When set again, and in position, pare the edges of the block square, and close to the object, set the knife—which should be quite dry—square and cut sections by moving the handle of the instrument rapidly in a lateral direction. A ribbon of sections is thus produced. (*See* Illustration.)

Fig. 9.
ROCKING MICROTOME.

The imbedded sections should be allowed to gently fall on to the surface of warm water in a flat dish, where they quickly flatten out, but still cohere at opposite edges. They can then be stained and mounted by special methods.

The Cambridge Rocking Microtome is automatic, and will cut sections from $\frac{1}{70000}$ of an inch to $\frac{1}{2500}$ of an inch in thickness; these figures of course, being only approximate. It can be obtained from the Cambridge Scientific Instrument Company, St. Tibb's Row, Cambridge; or Swift, of Tottenham Court Road.

Table of Tissues suitable for Imbedding in

GUM MUCILAGE.	CELLOIDIN.	PARAFFIN.
1. The majority of dental tissues, including all soft and softened organs.	1. Developmental tissues. 2. Decalcified fish's teeth. 3. Pulps *in situ*, especially those of molars and other large teeth.	1. Embryonic tissues, pulps, and peridental membrane, when serial sections are required.

CHAPTER VI.

On Staining and Mounting Sections.

The Advantages of Staining.
IN general histology it is found that unstained sections do not impart so much knowledge to the student as those specimens the structures of which have been differentiated by means of chemical stains or aniline dyes. It is necessary to colour the protoplasm of cells, and the outlines of fibrous tissues, because, otherwise, they would be lost in the general transparency of the section. In dental histology, however, many sections of the hard tissues, which have been prepared by grinding, are full of interesting information, even if they have not been subjected to the action of a dye. The histology of dentine and cementum is a case in point. But here the normal markings are rendered more or less prominent by the accumulation of detritus, water and air, which get into the interspaces of the tissues whilst grinding down the tooth specimen. Consequently, a preparation showing well-marked degrees of contrast—a study in blacks and greys, it might be termed—results.

Yet, in connection with the soft and hard dental tissues generally, it is all important to employ staining fluids, all sections having first been examined under the microscope, before the choice of stain is determined upon.

The various reagents used in microscopy may be classified as General and Specific.

The General Stains include all colouring matters that act on the plasma or ground-substance and nuclei of cells and tissues. They may therefore be spoken of as *Nuclear* and *Plasmatic*. No exclusively nuclear stain exists: the colouring of these parts of the cells depends on the comparatively greater affinity that some dyes have for them, than for the plasma in which they are imbedded.

Classification of Stains

The *Specific Stains* are those produced chiefly by the action of the salts of certain chemical compounds on certain tissues. Several aniline dyes are also included under this head.

Of all the general stains, the two most important are hæmatoxylene, and carmine, and their derivatives: and for all ordinary purposes the former is, beyond doubt, the more useful, either as a nuclear or as a plasmatic stain.

The two most valuable.

General Methods of Staining, Dehydration and Clearing.

Sections are removed from the preservative alcohol by means of a section lifter, and are dropped into a dish containing distilled water. Curled-up sections flatten out, twisted ones become unfolded, and presently thorough hydration takes place. A gentle stream of water from a glass pipette is useful for moving the objects about and washing them.

Washing.

(i.) *Staining by Immersion.*—Three watch glasses are placed on the table and half-filled with reagents. The first contains the staining solution, the second absolute alcohol, the third oil of cedar wood, or other clarifying medium. A glass capsule, of large dimensions, filled with distilled water, is also required.

Immersion.

The washed section is placed in the stain, in which it remains for a length of time variable according to the nature of the specimen and the character and strength of the stain used. When the object is completely coloured, it is lifted out on a section lifter and excess of colouring matter removed by well washing in distilled water.

Dehydration. It is now ready for dehydration, which is done by transferring the section to the watch-glass containing alcohol. After about three minutes immersion, the tissue is made to float on to a clean section lifter, which removes it from the alcohol.

Clearing. Allow excess of spirit to drop from off the lifter, and finally place the specimen in cedar wood oil. Leave it here about one to two minutes, this "clears" it, *i.e.*, renders it transparent. The action of the alcohol is to get rid of all water from the tissue, and make it fit for immersion in oil.

The section is finally removed from the clarifying medium, laid on a glass slide and immediately mounted.

For teased-out specimens. (ii.) *Staining by Transfusion.*—This plan is only adopted when certain tissues have been teased out, and are, therefore, not suitable for transference from reagent to reagent. Specimens of enamel prisms, sheaths of Neumann, isolated odontoblasts, &c., may all be stained by placing a small portion of the teased-out mass in the centre of a glass slide, and covering it with a drop or two of normal salt solution or glycerine, and a cover glass and applying an aqueous solution of borax-carmine, or rubine, to the side of the cover glass, by means of a glass rod. The dye immediately runs beneath, and soon stains the tissues, all excess being removed by means of blotting paper held to the opposite side of the cover glass.

It is then washed with distilled water to which a small quantity of a 1 per cent. solution of acetic acid has been added. More salt solution is added, and in this or in glycerine, the tissues are mounted, the cover glass being, at once, "rung" round with cement.

General Stains.

Of all the general stains, *Hæmatoxylene* is the most useful. There are numerous varieties of this stain—Ehrlich's, Delafield's, Kleinenberg's, Weigert's, &c., all differing in their formulæ. It is advisable, however, to make a point of using one kind for general purposes, and a special variety for special work. *Hæmatoxylene.*

The alcoholic solution of hæmatoxylene has, for its colouring principle, hæmatëin, and it may be used as a nuclear or as a plasmatic stain.

As a Nuclear Stain.—Place in a glass capsule 6 c.c. of distilled water, and add three or four drops of a strong, "ripened" alcoholic solution. Stir the mixture well. Place in the fluid three or four sections of soft or decalcified specimens. Leave them for a quarter or half-an-hour. Remove and wash thoroughly, first with distilled water, then ordinary (slightly alkaline) tap water. The stain is thus rendered free from precipitate,* and the nuclei are tinged a clear dark blue. *To Stain Cell Nuclei.*

Counter staining may be accomplished by dehydrating sections stained as above in absolute alcohol, to which an alcoholic solution of eosine has *Contrast Staining.*

---

* A heavy blue precipitate seems to form in most hæmatoxylenes, apparently due to conversion of alum into free sulphuric acid, and a basic compound of alumina. *See* Bolles Lee's Manual "Microtomist's Vade Mecum," 1893.

been added in sufficient quantity to deeply colour the absolute alcohol. The sections remain in the alcohol for two minutes, and are then passed through cedar wood oil, and mounted in Canada balsam. Thus most beautiful results are obtained. All kinds of developmental specimens are good objects for thus doubly staining in blue and red.

For Cell Protoplasm and Nuclei. To remove Overstaining.

As a Plasmatic Stain.—Proceed as just described, but leave sections in the hæmatoxylene from 18 to 24 hours. Do not counter-stain. Overstaining may be discharged by immersing sections in 70 per cent. alcohol to which one-tenth per cent. pure hydrochloric acid has been added. To neutralize the acidity of specimen, place it in a solution of bicarbonate of soda, 1 gr. to 2 oz., to prevent the subsequent fading of the stain.

Carmine.

Borax-Carmine is useful for staining in bulk, and as a nuclear or plasmatic stain.

Staining in Bulk.—For early embryonic jaws which are to be stained *en masse* and imbedded in celloidin, Grenacher's alcoholic solution of borax carmine is valuable.

Place the tissue in the stain for one to four days; remove to 70 per cent alcohol plus one-half per cent. of pure hydrochloric acid for one day; transfer to 90 per cent. alcohol for 24 hours, and finally keep in absolute alcohol before imbedding.

As a Nuclear and Plasmatic Stain.—Immerse sections in borax or lithium carmine for from half-an-hour to two hours. The stain may be removed from the ground substance of cells by placing in acidulated alcohol for ten minutes. Plasmatic stains are "fixed," by washing in one per cent. acetic acid in water for five minutes, and then washing in distilled water. Sections are afterwards dehydrated, cleared, and mounted in the usual way.

Fixing.

As a Contrast Stain to carmine alcoholic picric acid may be used. Treat the sections as just described, but do not place them in acidulated alcohol. After rinsing the sections for two minutes in 70 per cent. spirit, place them in picric acid for five minutes; then dehydrate, clear and mount. This combination is useful for sections of the pulp and the peridental membrane, the cells being stained pink and fibrous tissues yellow.

Contrast Staining.

Extremely beautiful effects may be obtained by staining vertical sections of fœtal jaws with teeth *in situ*—similar to those figured in Plates III. and VI.—with borax-carmine in the usual way, and counter-staining by immersing for a few minutes in an alcoholic solution of sulph-indigotate of soda. If this is done, the fibrous, connective, and other soft tissues are coloured violet, while bone and dentine are pink, and enamel (when present) a darker shade of pink. Another variation producing equally striking results occurs if eosine and methyl green are used in place of the carmine and indigo stains.

Additional combinations.

Other carmine stains comprise those known as Lithium and ammonium carmines, and Beale's, Merkel's, Orth's, and Grenacher's solutions. Advanced students are referred to the Appendix for details of these.

Other general stains are rubine, eosine, fuchsine, methylene blue, gentian violet, safranine, nigrosine, &c. These may be used as the fancy of the student dictates: for sections of decalcified teeth with the pulp *in situ*, the three first-named will be found of great value.[*]

Specific Stains.

These possess an affinity for certain elements in the tissues, and are used for demonstrating the out-

For what useful.

---

[*] Accidental staining of the fingers with aniline dyes may be removed by an application of soap and pumice.

lines of cells, nerve filaments, &c., either singly or combined with plasmatic stains.

In this group there may be mentioned, as suitable for dental microscopy, chloride of gold, osmic acid, chromic acid, salts of iron, and nitrate of silver.

Chloride of Gold.—This is an important reagent for differentiating the course of nerve fibres, and marking out the soft tissues in connection with dentine and cementum.

It is not necessary for the tissues to be absolutely fresh: those that have been previously hardened, and have passed through various stages of decalcification may be stained equally as well as any fresh section.

There are several methods in vogue, but the most convenient is that introduced by Mr. Underwood. He proceeds as follows:—

"*a*. Wash the sections in a solution of bicarbonate of soda. (5 grains to the ounce.)

"*b*. Put some 1 per cent. solution of chloride of gold in a watch-glass, test it with litmus paper, and, if it be acid, add bicarbonate of soda by drops till it is neutral; place the sections in the solution, and cover the watch glass with a lid to keep it in the dark—a lid of a china pot such as is used for potted meat serves very well—for from half-an hour to an hour, until the sections look straw coloured.

"*c*. Remove sections from staining fluid to distilled water, and leave them covered over—they must not be exposed to light for more than a few seconds—for a few minutes.

"*d*. Put some 1 per cent. solution of formic acid in a watch glass, float the glass in hot water, put the sections in the acid, cover them over, and keep them in the dark, and fairly hot, until they turn crimson. This generally takes about an hour, but the operator must be guided by the tint of the sections, which he must look at from time to time. A simple way to do this is to fill an old china anchovy-paste pot with hot water, place it on a stove, float the watch-glass containing the acid and the sections in it, and cover it up with its own lid.

"*e.* When stained, immerse the sections in cold distilled water for about half-an-hour.

"*f.* Dry the sections and mount them in glycerine jelly. Avoid Canada balsam."

During the manipulations with this and the following stains, it is advisable to use bone or wooden section lifters and other non-metallic instruments. It is not necessary to keep the bottle containing the gold solution in the dark.

Osmic Acid is valuable (i.) as a Specific (ii.) as a Pigmentation stain: for the former purpose, it is useful for colouring the myelin sheaths of spaces in medullated nerves; for the latter, the interglobular dentine. *Osmic Acid.*

(i.) Place a fresh isolated pulp in a one per cent. solution of this acid for 24 hours in the dark. Wash with distilled water, imbed in gum, cut sections, counter-stain with eosine if desired, dehydrate, clear, and mount.

(ii.) Ground-down sections of dentine are first stained, for a few minutes, in the ordinary solution of hæmatoxylene, and then partially decolourised by means of very dilute acetic acid, in such a manner that the interglobular spaces only retain the colour. Wash the sections in distilled water, and then place them in a one per cent. solution of osmic acid for one hour. Finally, wash, clear, and mount. Thus pigmentation of the interglobular spaces occurs, due, as Black has shown, to their being filled with a fine black amorphous deposit, which consequently renders them remarkably conspicuous.

Chromic Acid. — *Chromic Acid* can be used as an ⅛ per cent solution for staining the peripheral nerves in a fresh pulp (Boll).*

Iron. — *Iron and Tannin Stain.*—Place the section, after washing in distilled water, in a capsule containing liquor ferri perchloridi (B.P.) for twenty-four hours. Wash quickly in distilled water, and pass into a solution of tannic acid, 2 grains, and distilled water 6 c.c. for five or ten minutes. Remove and again wash in water.

Mr. Howard Mummery, in whose hands this iron stain has been very successful, has succeeded in tracing numerous fine fibres from the nerve bundles in the pulp.

Silver. — *Nitrate of Silver* is said to be of service for bringing out the epithelial nature of Nasmyth's membrane by staining black the intercellular cement substance of the tissue. A half per cent. solution in distilled water must be used, the membrane remaining in the stain for half-an-hour in the dark. After washing, it must be mounted in glycerine or Farrant's medium, and kept in the dark. This is the least useful of the specific stains.

Contrast Stains.

Other Contrast Stains. — In addition to those already mentioned, the following make good counter stains:—

Hæmatoxylene (Ehrlich's) and orange rubine.

Gentian violet and benzo-purpurine.

The Ehrlich-Biondi mixture—orange, fuchsine, and methyl green.

---

* Tomes' "Manual of Dental Anatomy," p. 45. 1894.

Borax-carmine (Merkel's) and borax-indigo-carmine.

For the last-named, use oxalic acid (a saturated aqueous solution) for washing sections. It fixes the indigo-carmine.

The above may be applied to specimens of developing tissues, pulp, and peridental membrane and dentine.

For double staining soft tissues *en masse*, combine alum-carmine with osmic acid.

Special Stains.

When it is necessary to investigate certain tissues during original research, it is most desirable to employ more than one method of staining. There are several special stains that are suited for dental work, and they must not be omitted here. A brief description of these special methods will be found useful.

Need for Special Stains.

Golgi's Stain.—There are three variations. The following is, however, convenient:—

Golgi's Stain

Place fresh sections of dentine in bichromate of potash (2 per cent. sol.) 8 parts, osmic acid (1 per cent. sol.) 2 parts, for 24 to 36 hours.

Remove to a ·5 per cent. solution of silver nitrate for one day. The tissues should be kept in the dark during the latter part of the process. Dehydrate, clear, and mount. Cover-glasses may be used.

Marchi's Method for staining degenerate nerve fibres. Applicable to sections of dental pulp. Pulps are hardened for a week in Müller's fluid, and then for another week in a solution composed of Müller's fluid two parts, osmic acid (1 per cent. sol.) one part. Large quantities of the solution should be used, and the tissues be very thin.

Marchi's Stain.

Weigert's Stain.

Weigert's Stain. — To blacken the medullated sheaths of nerves. Useful when pulps are prepared and cut *in situ*, having been previously hardened in bichromate of potash.

Sections are immersed in (i.) a saturated aqueous solution of acetate of copper with equal parts of water, kept at a temperature of 40° C. or 104° F. for two days. They are then washed in 90 per cent. alcohol and placed in (ii.) a fresh solution made after this formula :—

    Hæmatoxylene ... 1 part ...or 1 grm.
    Alcohol .... 10 parts ...or 10 c.c.
    Distilled Water ... 90 parts ...or 90 c.c.
    Saturated Sol. of Lithium Carb. 1 part or 1 c.c.

Leave in the solution for 24 hours. They are again washed in distilled water for many hours, and finally decolourised in two hours by placing in (iii) a solution of

    Borax .... 2 parts or 2 grms.
    Potassium Ferricyanide 2½ parts or 2·5 grms.
    Water .... 200 parts or 200 c.c.

Subsequently they are washed, dehydrated and mounted in the usual manner.

Charters White's Stain.

Charters White's Stain. — This method has for its object the differentiation of internal cavities and spaces in bone and teeth. It produces very beautiful specimens of the calcified tissues. Cut teeth into sections, having the thinness of about $\frac{1}{25}$ of an inch. Soak them in absolute alcohol for a short time, then place them in ether sulph. meth. Make a stained celloidin solution by adding fuchsine to alcohol "until a dark port wine colour is produced," mixing this with ether and adding celloidin till the required consistency is reached. Saturate the sections with this mixture for several days. Remove them and let them dry by evaporation. Finish by grinding on a wheel, and rubbing between plates of glass; and mount at once in balsam.

Dehydrating Tissues.

An immersion of two minutes' duration in absolute alcohol will thoroughly rid ordinary sections of all water, after they have been stained, and before "clearing." Very delicate tissues, however, shrink too much if placed at once in absolute alcohol. Therefore it is necessary, when dealing with these cases, to pass sections quickly through 50 per cent., 70 per cent., and 90 per cent. spirit, before finally immersing in absolute alcohol. *Special Dehydration.*

Clearing Sections.

Several essential oils are used for this purpose, including the oils of cedar wood, cloves, bergamot, origanum, and also xylol or turpentine. Their functions are twofold—first, to render stained sections transparent, and second, to prepare them for the balsamic mounting media. *Clearing.*

The object is removed from absolute alcohol, and floated on to the surface of the oil in a watch-glass. It should remain in the oil for 1-2 minutes.

A newer and better plan is to put the clearing medium into a test tube, and carefully pour on its surface a quantity of absolute alcohol. Place the sections in the alcohol; they will shortly have sunk to the bottom of the test tube through the alcohol, which may then be drawn off by means of a glass pipette. Sections are then ready for mounting. *Another Method.*

Oil of cloves must not be used for clearing celloidin-imbedded sections. It removes aniline dyes and causes a certain amount of shrinkage. Oil of bergamot clears celloidin, and does not dissolve it. *Special Precaution.*

Table of Tissues suitable for Staining with

1. Hæmatoxylene and its varieties	All embryonic and fœtal soft tissues, pulp, peridental membrane, gum, &c.
2. Carmine and its varieties	The same; and also enamel prisms, dentinal fibrils in young dentine, interglobular spaces. Fish's teeth.
3. Fuchsine	Ramifications of dentinal tubules, cemental canaliculi, and the spaces in osseous tissue, &c.
4. Rubine, methylene blue, eosine, etc.	Dental pulp; and peridental membrane, striæ of Retzius, dentine, dental gum.
5 Double stains as Ehrlich-Biondi fluid	Developmental tissues.
6. Gold chloride ... (Underwood's plan)	Interglobular spaces, odontoblasts *in situ*, nerves of pulp, dentinal fibrils, interprismatic enamel substance (Böjecker).
7. Osmic acid ...	Medullated nerves of pulp, interglobular spaces.
8. Chromic acid ...	The same.
9. Iron and tannin ...	Dentinal fibrils, nerves of pulp.
10. Nitrate of silver...	Nasmyth's membrane; and as Golgi's stain — sheaths of Neumann *in situ*, interglobular spaces, layer of semi-calcified dentine.

MOUNTING SECTIONS.

The final stages of practical microscopy are concerned with the operations of permanently mounting sections, and "finishing" slides by cementing their cover glasses in such a manner that evaporation of the mountant cannot take place.

Reasons for using the Flotation Method.

There are two chief methods by which sections may be mounted, *viz.*, (A) Transference with a section lifter, and (B) Flotation. The former is the one more generally employed, being applicable to the majority of specimens which are to be preserved in Canada balsam, or other media. Mounting by flotation is used when the sections are too thin or small or friable to be moved from reagent to reagent, as in the first method; and when they are to be mounted in aqueous media.

A

Mounting by Transference.

Sections having been stained, washed, dehydrated, and cleared, as already indicated, are removed from the watch glass of cedar oil, by passing a clean section lifter underneath them. Holding the blade horizontally with a considerable amount of oil and the section upon it, the student carries the section to a clean slide laid flat on the surface of a sheet of white paper lying on the table, and slightly tilts the lifter allowing the section, enveloped in oil, to run on to the slide, and guiding it with a needle-point towards the centre. Excess of oil is removed by tilting the slide and carefully absorbing what remains, by means of a piece of clean thin blotting or filter paper. A drop of benzole balsam from the end of a glass rod, is next placed on the top of the section, and a cover glass, which must be thoroughly clean and dry, having received a drop of the same medium on its reverse side (that is, the side which will shortly touch the slide) is gently lowered on to the section in the following way :— *Use of a Section Lifter. Mounting in Balsam.*

Method of applying the Cover Glass.—Hold the cover glass by its periphery, between the left forefinger and thumb in a tilted position; pass beneath it a needle, and gradually bring the needle closer and closer to the slide till the drops of medium have met. (*See* fig. 10). Then slowly remove the needle and the *To avoid air bubbles.*

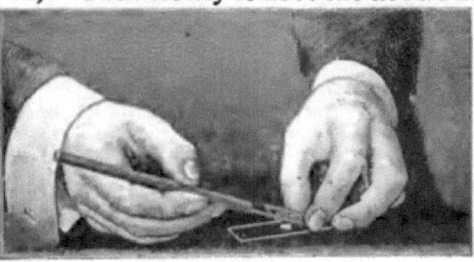

Fig. 10.

mountant will gradually fill the whole of the under surface of the cover glass, at the same time that it excludes a ring of air from its centre. This method of placing the cover glass in position is applicable to both aqueous and balsamic mounting media, and with a little practice, it is thus possible to prevent any air bubbles from being retained between the glasses.

Removal of air bubbles.

Should they, however, be present, the balsam should be slowly warmed over a spirit flame, and a mounting clip passed over the centres of both cover glass and slide. The clip should remain in place for a few days.

If it is found after a section has been mounted, that an insufficient quantity of balsam has been used, and that air *spaces* exist beneath the cover glass, it is best not to warm the slide, but to apply a drop or two of thin balsam to the slide, near that edge of the cover glass where the space is seen. The balsam by capillary attraction runs beneath the cover glass, and efficiently fills the vacuum. In a week or two the mountant will be dry and the slide can then be "rung."

Final treatment.

Any superfluous balsam that may have been pressed from beneath the cover glass during or after mounting, should not be removed until quite dry. If a penknife is used for scraping it away, and the edge of the cover glass finally wiped with a clean rag, moistened with xylol, the slide will present a neat appearance.

Other Methods of Mounting in Balsam.

(1.) *For Calcified Tissues.*—Dried, ground-down sections of teeth can be mounted in Canada balsam without previous dehydration or clearing, the object here being the retention of air and water in the dentinal tubules and other spaces. The highly refractive balsam should not be thin enough to allow of its penetration into these spaces, or the structure of the hard tissues will become obliterated. For attaining this end, the plan of Mr. Charters White* is to be recommended.

Charters White's Method. The tooth having been ground while fastened on to the slide with Canada balsam, is unloosed from its position by long immersion in absolute alcohol, which may be wiped off with a camel's hair brush. When quite clean, the section should be placed for a long period in distilled water till complete hydration occurs. The surfaces of the section should be then quickly dried on a clean thin cloth, and the specimen mounted in stiff balsam. The water and air in the dentinal tubules will thus prevent the balsam entering them.

Mr. J. E. Ady† adopts for the same purpose the following mode of procedure:—

Ady's Method. Finished sections are dipped for a moment in an alcoholic solution of white shellac, "and withdrawn when a thin coating of the lac is left over its surface, occluding the spaces." They are then mounted in usual way.

A plan has been devised by Mr. Mansbridge‡ for giving the same results. He says:—

Mansbridge's Method. "Take a clean slide, place it upon a hot table with a small single lump of (desiccated) balsam upon it: use sufficient heat to slowly melt the balsam, which must not be made too hot. When sufficiently fluid, lay the section upon it, and cover with a hot cover glass, which must be pressed down in such a way as to expel the air from beneath it. Remove

---
* *Op. cit.* pp. 41 & 42.   † *Idem.* p. 42.
‡ Transactions Odontological Society. Vol. xxv., p. 176.

the slide to a cool surface and continue to keep pressure upon the cover glass for a few minutes, when the balsam will be found to be quite hard."

(2.) *For Decalcified Tissues.* — Air may be well retained in interglobular spaces, tubules, &c., by treating sections of teeth with the method that Prof. Flemming* recommends for decalcified bone.

Flemming's Method.
They should be washed with alcohol and ether and laid flat on glass, and then covered with a double layer of blotting paper under a heavy piece of glass. They can then be dried in the air, or better and more quickly in an oven. A glass slide having been prepared by putting a drop of warmed stiff balsam in the centre, and allowing it to spread out flat, receives the dried section. It is then covered with a similarly prepared cover glass, a clip is applied, and the slide and section warmed over a spirit flame.

To remove the thick, hard, and perhaps dirty Canada balsam that sometimes occludes the clear interspaces of sections prepared by Weil's process. *Mr. Sydney Spokes* suggests the following :—

Spokes' Method.
If the section has been sufficiently ground, it is well washed with water and scrubbed with a camel's hair pencil. Next, it is placed in the centre of a glass slide covered from dust, and allowed to dry. When about to mount the section, the student should have ready at hand a clean cover glass with a drop of warm balsam in the centre. Then upon this section —which has not been moved from its position on the slide—must be dropped a succession of drops of chloroform, one drop at a time in such a manner that at no time does the chloroform become completely evaporated, or the section curled by drying. The

---

* Zeit. f. Wiss. Mik. 1886. p. 47.

solvent action of the chloroform will cause small *débris* to be thus finally floated to the circumference of the section without the parts being disturbed in their mutual relationship. Before the last drop of chloroform has evaporated the cover-glass should be inverted and lowered gradually on to the specimen, in the way already described.

B

Mounting by Flotation.

The section, stained or otherwise, having been finally washed, is placed in a large dish of clean water, where it is flattened out, if necessary, by gently removing the creases or folds with a camel's hair brush.

A thoroughly clean slide is held between the fore- *Modus* finger and thumb of the left hand at an angle of *operandi.* about 60°, and dipped for half its length in the water. The section is guided into the centre of the slide by means of careful manipulation with a mounted needle held in the left hand. If one end of the slide is tilted up a little further, and the needle point fixes the section in position, the slide may be entirely withdrawn from the water, with the section lying flat upon its surface. Excess of water must be removed by the application of a piece of blotting paper to the side of the section as the slide lies on the table top. A drop of an aqueous mountant having been put on the section, a cover glass is applied, and the mounting completed.

Ordinary sections that are to be mounted in aqueous media are not necessarily always treated with the flotation process. In many cases the section is lifted out of the washing water and simply placed on the slide by means of a section lifter.

Aqueous Mountants.

The Aqueous Mountants include, among others, glycerine jelly, Farrant's medium, normal salt solution, and soluble glass. Sections which are to be mounted in any of these fluids do not require dehydrating or clarifying, the media themselves performing these functions at the time of using. The two first named are the most useful.

Glycerine Jelly is of service for mounting sections stained with chloride of gold, and for teased-out specimens, such as sheaths of Neumann, &c. It consists of French gelatine, glycerine, and distilled water, in the proportion of one, four, and six parts respectively. The slide, mountant, and cover glass should be slightly warmed, and the slide "rung" with cement as soon afterwards as practicable.

Similar in properties, but dissimilar in composition, is *Farrant's Medium*, which consists of glycerine, powdered gum arabic, and a saturated solution of arsenious acid.

Normal Salt Solution is a valuable mountant after specimens have been stained by transfusion. It should be allowed to run under the cover glass after excess of the stain has been washed away.

Soluble Glass has been found to be a fairly successful mountant by the writer. It does not possess any very special qualifications, and the foregoing media are certainly more reliable.

It is a mistake to mount more than one section on each slide, unless they are *extremely* thin.

Special Methods of Mounting.

Special slides for ribbon sections.

For sections which have been cut in paraffin, and are to be arranged in series, special slides and cover glasses must be purchased. The former should measure 6 by 1 or 2 inches, and the latter 5 by ¾-inch or 1½ inches. The sections are placed on a dry slide, one after the other, or in a ribbon, and the slide tilted to allow excess of water to drain away, ten minutes being necessary for this. When nearly dry, drop some creosote-shellac on the section and place the slide over a water bath for 24 hours. Dissolve the paraffin off with xylol, and the sections will be adherent to the glass. Clear them with oil of cedar, and mount in Canada balsam. Another way is to put a drop of water and spirit on each section, and evaporate carefully over a spirit lamp. Then use xylol, &c.

Unmounting Sections.

It is sometimes necessary to remove a mounted section from the slide, and re-stain, and re-mount it. This applies chiefly to sections which, having been kept some length of time, have faded, **and to those** for which **a wrong stain has been used.** Tissues dyed with hæmatoxylene, no **matter how carefully it has been done, lose, in the course of years, a great deal of their beauty and their brilliancy.**

Need for unmounting.

If care is exercised, these old sections can be renovated with much success.

The process will vary with the **nature of the mountant.**

(i.) *Those Mounted in Canada Balsam.*—First remove the cementing ring around the cover glass, by soaking the whole slide in a small quantity of ether. A **sharp fine knife** point will **then** scratch off the rest of the dissolved cement. The centre of the slide **should next** be held over a spirit flame, or placed on a hot brass table. Heat must be applied gradually and at once stopped on any signs of bubbling of the balsam becoming noticed. Before the slide and cover glass have become cold again, gently push the latter towards the side of the slide, and carefully lift it up with a pair of fine tweezers. Dissolve off the rest of the balsam by immersing the slide with the section still adherent, in a bath of chloroform or xylol for five or ten minutes. The specimen is then removed from the slide by means of a small stiff brush, and placed on a clean glass slip and examined quickly microscopically, to ascertain if it has suffered by removal. If not, float it off on to distilled water where it should be well washed for an hour. Then re-stain and mount in the ordinary manner.

(ii.) *Those Mounted in Aqueous Media.*—Place the whole slide in a tray of hot water for about one minute. The heat will dissolve the mountant, and at the same time loosen the cover glass, which should not be lifted up, but gently pushed along the surface of the slide.

Finishing Slides.

It is often quite unnecessary to "ring" balsam preparations, though a black cement neatly applied, always gives a slide a finished appearance. It is imperative, however, to cement cover glasses having beneath them glycerine jelly, or Farrant's solution.

Use of a turntable. Fix the slide on a turntable, by means of the clips, in such a position that the centres of cover glass and the brass table correspond. Revolve the disc with the left forefinger, and apply the medium with a long thin camel's hair brush, a Rigger, No. 1, being best for this purpose. The brush can afterwards be washed with turpentine or soap and hot water.

About Cements. There are many cements made and sold for "ringing" slides—Aspinall's black enamel gives very satisfactory results,—black being preferred, because white or coloured cements soon begin to look dirty, and a fresh "ring" has to be applied.

Finally, a neat white label is affixed to one end of the slide, and the character of the specimen, the name of the stain, and mountant, and date noted thereon, the slide being subsequently placed in the cabinet.

The student is advised to purchase his staining solutions, mountants, and cements ready made. They can be obtained of Messrs. Becker and Co., of Hatton Wall, Kanthack, of Golden Square, and all opticians and dealers in microscopical materials.

CHAPTER VII.

ON THE INJECTION OF CAPILLARIES, AND ON THE MEASUREMENT AND DELINEATION OF OBJECTS.

Though falling outside the scope of dental microscopy, the injection of the blood vessels of organs is of great interest to the enthusiastic student. The study of the relationship which exists between the vascular supply and the dental tissues themselves is also of importance, since it may throw occasional light on the causes of deviations or aberrations from, and suppressions of, certain typical forms. This study cannot be followed without a knowledge of the methods of injecting the vessels.

Natural and Artificial Injections.

Vascular injection may be either natural or artificial: by the former is implied the retention of blood corpuscles within the capillary walls—best observed in sections of fish's teeth (vaso-dentine), the pulps of which have been hardened in Müller's fluid, and cut *in situ* [*see* Plate VIII., Fig. 3]. Artificial injection means the method of filling the vessels with an extraneous medium.

This medium may have for its basis water, glycerine, or gelatine combined with a colouring matter. When employing fluids, of which gelatine is the vehicle, it is necessary that the animal should be kept at the temperature of the body throughout the manipulations: and this is obviously inconvenient. For dental work, perhaps, the most suitable method is the following:—

Modus operandi.

Procure a small animal, such as a kitten, or rabbit, and subject it to the vapours of chloroform, in which a capsule containing three minims of nitrite of amyl has been crushed.

Preparation of the Animal.

Immediately after death, lay it on its back, and fasten its stretched out limbs on to a board, which should be placed in a large shallow tray. Remove the sternum with its attachments, and expose the pericardium. Snip this through with scissors, and finally cut off the apex of the heart, opening up the right and left ventricles.

On a shelf, at the height of five or six feet above the table, place two Wulff's bottles, one containing an abundant supply of warm normal salt solution, and the other the injection mass, made according to the following formula:*

Pure Glycerine	4 ounces.
Tincture of Sesquichloride of Iron ...	20 drops.
Ferrocyanide of Potassium	6 grains.
Strong Hydrochloric acid	5 drops.
Water	2 ounces.

To a syphon, in each of the bottles, attach a piece of long, thin, flexible, india-rubber tubing, which has been previously rinsed through with a stream of water. On the free end of each tube fasten a stopcock. Exhaust the air in the dependent tubes by suction, thus causing a stream of salt solution in the one, and of injection fluid in the other. Stop the flow by turning off the stopcocks. The weight of fluid in the two tubes will insure a continuous and uniform flow through the blood

---

*This is a slight modification of Dr. Beale's Prussian blue solution, as suggested by Mr. Charters White.

vessels of the animal, this being sufficient to overcome the normal resistance of their walls.

Pass the nozzle of an injection syringe, through the left ventricle of the heart, into the orifice of the arch of the aorta, and, when in position, tie it firmly to the vessel walls by passing a threaded ligature needle underneath and around it. Insert the stop-cock attached to the tube, containing the saline solution, into the nozzle, avoiding the entrance of air, and turn the tap. The fluid should immediately commence to flow into the arterial system, and at the end of about half-an-hour run out with a clear stream from the right ventricle, showing that it has circulated through the whole of the arteries, capillaries, and veins of the animal. Again avoiding the entrance of air, rapidly substitute the second for the first stop-cock, and the gradual diminution of the injection mass in the Wulff's bottle will denote the rate at which permeation of the blood vessels is taking place. Examine the tongue and conjunctivæ of the animal, and, when they assume a bluish tinge, the operation may be stopped. On the completion of injection, turn off the stop-cock, ligature the artery, tying a reef knot, and remove the nozzle. Finally, lay the animal in a deep dish of cold water for an hour. Excise the mandible, divide it at the symphysis, and place the halves, after further division, in Müller's fluid till they are hardened. Complete the process by immersing the pieces in alcohol, afterwards decalcify if necessary, imbed in gum mucilage, and cut on an ether-freezing microtome. Stain the sections with carmine.

There are two points of importance to notice in connection with the injection of the blood-vessels of *young* animals. First, during the act of excising the sternum and its attachments, unless great care

Washing out the Vessels.

Their Injection.

Final Treatment.

Precautions.

is exercised, the knife will open the large venous trunks lying closely behind the manubrium sterni. It is well, therefore, to allow the sterno-clavicular articulations to remain. Secondly, it is very easy, when tying the reef knot, to draw the ligature so tightly that it cuts completely through the delicate walls of the aorta, with the result of spoiling the whole operation. Otherwise the method is quite simple, but nevertheless very successful.

The Measurement of Objects.

It is often convenient, in giving descriptions of histological specimens, to be able to make a note of the dimensions, as well as the shape and general appearance of the object. This would be very difficult without an acquaintance with the several methods which have been devised. The size of cells, distance between dentinal tubules, length and width of interglobular or other spaces, etc., may be obtained by using a stage-micrometer, singly or else combined with either a camera lucida, or an ocular micrometer.

The Stage Micrometer.

This consists simply of an ordinary glass slide, ruled at its centre with microscopic, diamond-cut lines, which are separated from each other by fractions of an inch or millimeter. The stage micrometer alone almost suffices for measuring objects, but, if used in combination with a neutral tint reflector or eyepiece micrometer, it will form a very valuable adjunct to the student's microscopical outfit. *Instrument for Measuring Objects.*

The lines on the slide are equidistant, and are either hundredths or thousandths of an inch apart in the English form, or tenths or hundredths of a millimeter in the Continental model, and when focussed and viewed as a transparent object, they appear sharp and clear in the field of vision.

Method of Using.—Put the microscope in a vertical position, with the specimen on the stage. Focus the latter and by keeping both eyes open, observe its faint image thrown on to a piece of white paper, lying on one side of the microscope on the table. Without moving the position of the eyes, trace the outline with a pencil. Remove the slide, substitute for it a stage micrometer, still keeping both eyes open, and the lines will appear faintly drawn across the sketch. Point off these lines with a pencil and rule them across. Note the combination of ocular and objective, the height of the eyepiece above the paper, and the extent to which the draw-tube has been drawn out. Calculate the size of the cell by computing the number of spaces it occupies between the lines, the distance of which is known.

This is, at best, but a rough method of measuring the size of objects. More trustworthy data can be obtained by using a stage micrometer with a camera lucida or tint reflector. Beale's neutral tint reflector is a small circle of tinted glass mounted in a metal frame, and attached, by means of an arm at an angle, to a ring which is intended to be slipped over the tube of the eyepiece. The reflector does not magnify the object, but when in position, it projects the image on to a piece of white paper.

Beale's Tint Reflector.

The Stage Micrometer and Reflector Combined.

Method of Using.—The micrometer is fixed on the centre of the stage, and the microscope tilted horizontally, having the reflector at an angle of 45° to the eye lens of the ocular. If the micrometer is

MEASUREMENT OF OBJECTS.

well illuminated, and the observer's eye looks from above through the reflector, the lines will be seen projected on the paper underneath. These lines should be measured and pencil marks made on the paper, to be ultimately ruled in pen and ink. By subdividing the lines, thousandths or other greater fractions of an inch can be estimated, and these again converted into millimeters or micromillimeters, according to the following scale:—

  1 centimeter (cm) = 10 millimeters.
  1 millimeter (mm) = 1,000 micromillimeters (μ).
  25 micromillimeters (25μ) = $\frac{1}{1000}$ of an inch (approximately).

Micrometer Chart. The distance between the centre of the eye-lens of the ocular and the paper being known, it is not a difficult thing for the student to make a chart bearing these lines upon it.

Thus:—If a ¼ inch objective and C ocular are used, and the paper is lying on a plane distant five inches from the centre of the eye-lens of the ocular, then on the paper—

  $\frac{1}{100}$ inch will measure three inches nearly.
  $\frac{1}{1000}$ inch will measure $\frac{3}{10}$ inch nearly.

The micrometer having now been removed from the microscope stage, and the section inserted in its place, it is only necessary to sketch in pencil the outlines of cells, distances between dentinal tubules, on the chart, over the lines, to easily make the desired measurements. These should only be taken at the centre of the disc of light thrown on the paper.

The Ocular Micrometer.

Another Method. A still more easy and reliable method is to employ a stage and eyepiece micrometer together, the microscope body being, in this instance, kept in an upright position. The ocular micrometer consists of a single circle of glass, the scale of which is divided into hundredths of an inch. It is made to slip into the eyepiece between the lens and field glasses. If this is used instead of the tint reflector, two sets of lines will appear in the field of vision. When in focus, it is first necessary to determine how many divisions of the ocular micrometer occupy one space of the stage micrometer. The proportion they bear to each other must be noted, and when the section is placed on the stage and focussed, the size of its cells, or other constituents, can be estimated by remembering that so many of the lines seen over the section equal $\frac{1}{100}$ of an inch.

The Delineation of Objects.

The ability to reproduce on paper the chief features of his sections will be of great service to the student during his study of dental histology. Some workers can make drawings of their preparations with great ease, by mere inspection of their structure through the microscope; but the majority find this a difficult matter, and it certainly requires long practice before anything like perfection is reached.

Instruments for Drawing Specimens. But, by employing a camera lucida, or Beale's reflector, as already hinted, useful sketches of the tissues may, with a little trouble, be made by anyone.

Method of using. The arrangement of apparatus is similar to that just described,—the microscope horizontally fixed, the reflector in position in front of the eyepiece, and the section well illuminated by means of lamplight. The intensity of the illuminant should be modified until a point is attained at which the image, seen through the reflector, is at its best.

There has, however, always been a certain amount of difficulty attending the use of the camera lucida, or Beale's neutral tint reflector, for the purpose of making microscopical drawings. The twisting of the head into an uncomfortable position, the great fatigue to the eyes, and the by-no-means easy task of viewing both image and pencil at the same time, add to the troubles of making a faithful reproduction of the object on paper.

Alternative Method.

To those especially, who do not possess a camera lucida, or Beale's instrument, and to students generally, the following arrangement of ordinary apparatus may be recommended:—The microscope body is placed in a horizontal position, and the mirror removed from its sub-stage attachment. The microscopic slide having been placed on the stage, the illuminant (lamplight for choice) is "condensed" on to the slide by means of a "bull's-eye," in the same way as for photo-micrography. Care must be taken to "centre" the light. A concave mirror is then attached to the front of the eye-piece of the microscope by a piece of thin wood or a spring, having its surface at an angle of about 45° with the plane of the eye-lens of the ocular. The image is thus projected on to the paper beneath. No distortion will occur if the outer ring of light is *perfectly* circular. A dark cloth, such as photographers use, is thrown over the draughtsman's head and the body of the microscope, and all light excluded save that which passes through the microscope lenses. Any section can thus be easily, rapidly, and comfortably drawn, and fairly accurate representations obtained of objects magnified up to 500-600 diameters.

CHAPTER VIII.

ON PHOTO-MICROGRAPHY.

Use of Diagrams.

THE drawing of an object made with the help of a camera lucida, or reflector, is obviously in many respects incomplete, no matter how skilful the draughtsman may be. Such a diagram is not useless, for its chief points being brought into prominence, by this very lack of detail, its clearness may be more serviceable for teaching purposes than would an elaborate reproduction. But when an exact copy of a section is required the outline sketch fails, and the application to microscopy of photographic processes can alone produce the desired effect. Photo-micrography is the term applied to the art by which enlarged images of microscopic specimens are permanently recorded.

And of Photo-micrography.

It is not possible, in a work like the present, to give a complete account of photo-micrography. The writer's aim, therefore, is merely to detail methods of working by which the beginner may obtain satisfactory negatives and pictures of his dental sections. To amateur photographers the combination of photography and microscopy will be simple; but those who have no knowledge of the former will, at first, find it beset with many difficulties.

The subject may be considered under two heads, (A) a description of the necessary apparatus, and (B) methods of operating.

A.

Photographic Apparatus.

The room which the student intends to devote to photo-micrography should, if possible, be provided with arrangements both for taking photographs and developing plates. Spacious and well-ventilated, it should be situated in such a position in the house that no vibrations due to disturbances out of doors can affect the instruments, rigidity of apparatus giving freedom from tremor being a *sine quâ non*. Some workers prefer a concrete floor on which to place their tables. All windows should be fitted with wooden frames which are covered over with two or three thicknesses of orange or ruby coloured medium. The doors should close in such a manner as to exclude all light. A firm deal table, measuring about seven feet long by two or three feet wide, standing in the centre of the room, supports the baseboard of the camera at the height of three or four feet from the floor. There should also be a plentiful supply of cold water, a large table on which to place the developing and other dishes, and a dark room lamp. *Fittings of Room.*

A very important piece of apparatus is the photo-micrographic *camera*. This is not of the usual form, but has a long bellows body. It should be adapted for taking either ¼-plate or ½-plate negatives—*i.e*, pictures measuring $3\frac{1}{4} \times 4\frac{1}{4}$ inches, or $6\frac{1}{2} \times 4\frac{3}{4}$ inches. The accompanying figure illustrates its chief parts. *Description of Camera.*

Fig. 11.

COMPLETE PHOTO-MICROGRAPHIC APPARATUS,
SHEWING THE ADJUSTMENT OF THE PARTS.

The bellows body extends 30 inches or more, on a mahogany baseboard, which has a scale let into it so that the distance between the objective and plate may be accurately known, and the desired amplification of the object readily ascertained. The microscope, illuminant, and paralleliser (bull's-eye condenser) are placed on a projecting board at the fore part of the camera, the sliding front of which allows any microscope to be fitted to it. A rod running from back to front of the apparatus is attached to the grooved milled head of the fine adjustment of the microscope by means of a thin india-rubber ring, and allows fine focussing to be done when the student is standing at the back of the camera. A dark slide with two carriers for ¼ plate negatives, and three masks—circular, square, and oval, for making neat pictures, comprise the rest of the camera outfit.*

Lenses.

Any good *microscope* may be employed for photo-micrographic purposes. The advantages derived from the use of apochromatic lenses† are very great,

---

* The ingenious student can make, with the expenditure of but little time and money, a camera suited in most respects for all his requirements.

† In apochromatic objectives, the fringe of colour, or other aberration of light, seen in the field when ordinary lenses are used, is practically abolished.

but objectives that have not been specially manufactured for photographic work may be used, and will yield excellent results.

If the actinic (photographic) and visual foci are not perfectly coincident, they can be "corrected" at a small cost by any competent optician.

The **oxy-hydrogen limelight is by far the best** *illuminant*, as the light which passes through the objective emanates from a mere point (approximately); but the student will find a paraffin microscopic lamp with a flat wick very serviceable, especially if a small piece of camphor is placed in the oil, to render the light whiter and more actinic. *Source of Lighting.*

A bull's-eye condenser **throws very** nearly parallel rays of light on the section, and if centrally placed, illuminates it uniformly.

It is advisable not to use an eyepiece, the chief objections being a great restriction of the field of view, and marked loss of light.

The accessory apparatus needed are glass stoppered bottles to hold the developing and toning solutions, a graduated glass measure, three or four ½-plate porcelain developing dishes, and a larger one to contain the "fixing" solution, and also several printing-frames. *Other Apparatus*

B

Methods of Operating.

Preliminary Steps.—Having already placed a box of sensitive dry plates on the table and opened the dark slide, the student should light the dark room lamp, and turn the flame down so low as to give only a very faint illumination. Then standing some distance from the light, he should, as quickly as possible, put a sensitive plate in one of the carriers of the dark slide. The edges only of the plate must *Placing Plates in the Slide.*

be touched, and its shiny non-sensitive side lie uppermost when in position in the carrier. In the course of time it becomes quite easy to transfer the plates to the slide in absolute darkness, a touch of the fingers at one extreme corner of the plate indicating which is its film side. If this transference is accomplished in the dark, so much the better, as there is then no risk whatever of "fogging" or injuring the sensitiveness of the film. The operation is repeated with a second plate, and the dark slide tightly shut and wrapped for a few moments in a black photographer's cloth.

Kinds of Plates.

The plates specially recommended for photomicrography are Edwards' "Isochromatic Instantaneous," or the Ilford "Isochromatic Medium" for using with stained sections. Ilford "Ordinary" plates answer remarkably well for unstained objects.

Arrangement of Instruments. — The body of the microscope is placed horizontally and the eye-piece removed. A piece of thin dull black or brown paper is then inserted in the draw-tube, to prevent the production of what is technically known as a "flare" on the sensitive plate. The draw-tube is fitted firmly to the front of the camera, the microscope stand being securely fixed to the projecting portion of the base board. The lamp is then brought into position; and the wick having been trimmed to make the edges of the flame parallel, it is placed opposite the substage condenser, with one edge of the flame turned towards it, in such a manner that the long axis of the flame and the optical axis of the microscope coincide—the centre of the flame exactly corresponding with the centre of the field-lens of the objective. The mirror should be turned aside, and the substage condenser used with high power objectives only. The student is recommended to employ

Illuminant.

nothing but his 1-inch objective, until the initial difficulties have been overcome. A bull's-eye con- *Condensing the Light.* denser is now interposed between the illuminant and the section which has been clamped on to the stage of the microscope; it is then centralized, and the whole section evenly illuminated. The importance of centralization cannot be too much insisted upon. An examination of the ground-glass screen of the camera will show whether the lighting of the object is uniform; if it is not, the focus of the paralleliser must be altered, till the desired degree of brightness and uniformity is attained. The camera bellows are finally extended to the necessary distance, and a suitable mask placed in the end of the camera, so that the enlarged aërial image of the section is projected on the screen in the required form. Focussing is the next step: and this is accom- *Focussing.* plished by slowly turning the long focussing rod. When the image appears well defined, the ground-glass screen should be removed, and replaced by a piece of transparent glass, ruled with diamond cut lines, and a magnifier used to make certain that every portion of the image is perfectly clear and sharp. The circular edge of the image may appear out of focus; this will necessitate the employment of a diaphragm which will cut off the scattered rays of light, and give it a better definition. To counteract the diminution of intensity of the light, a longer exposure must be given.

Exposure.—The student having satisfied himself *To prevent Blurring.* with the sharpness of the image, must exclude the passage of all light through the microscope by means of a thick screen of black cardboard, which is to be placed between the lamp and bull's-eye, or section and objective if there is room. This being done, the dark slide containing the sensitive plates is substituted for the glass screen, care being taken not to shake the instruments; the shutter is opened and one plate exposed by removing the cardboard screen. *Fig.* 11 shews the arrangement of camera and microscope when this stage has been reached.

Exposure.

The exact duration of exposure required to produce a strong negative is very difficult, at first, to estimate. No hard and fast rules can be laid down, though many attempts have been made; the student's carefully recorded experience will prove to be the only sure guide. The author has obtained excellent negatives by using Edwards' "Instantaneous Isochromatic" plates under the following conditions:—

Camera extended 24 inches, 1 inch objective used, no substage condenser, no diaphragm, ordinary lamplight: for hæmatoxylene stained sections—*exposure ten seconds*: for sections somewhat feebly stained with carmine—*twenty-six seconds.*

Ilford "Isochromatic Medium" plates will require under circumstances similar to those first named, 20 to 50 seconds, and Ilford "Ordinary," 4 to 10 seconds. It may also be stated that the image projected by a $\frac{1}{6}$-inch objective will require an exposure of 50 to 60 seconds, and $\frac{1}{12}$-inch oil immersion, 3 to 6 minutes. The beginner will be much assisted in his judgment of the proper length of exposure, by first experimenting with a few plates. He may adopt this plan:—

To obtain approximate duration of Exposure.

The shutter of the dark slide, on being drawn out a short distance, will allow only a portion of the plate to be influenced by the action of the light. This exposure must be timed in seconds by a watch. The shutter should be further opened and the time again noted, and the operation repeated at intervals of 5 or 10 seconds, till the whole of the plate is exposed. On subsequent development *one* portion of the negative will probably be seen to have been correctly exposed, and the right length of time to give to similar sections thus ascertained.

Developing Negatives.—The plate having been exposed for the correct length of time, the cardboard screen must be again used to shut off rays of light, and the shutter of the dark slide immediately closed. The microscope lamp is then turned out, and the room faintly illuminated by the light from the ruby lamp. The negative is carefully removed from the dark slide and placed filmside uppermost in a developing dish, and then flooded with a developing solution. *[Removal of Plate.]*

Of developers there are many kinds—pyrogallic acid combined with soda or ammonia salts, hydroquinone, metol, amidol, &c. The formula given for use with Ilford plates is good, the only objections being that it stains the fingers if used carelessly, and it does not retain its properties for any long period of time. A stock solution consisting of pyrogallic acid 1 ounce and water 6 ounces, with the addition of 20 drops of nitric acid should have been previously prepared, and two separate solutions, made as follows, contained in labelled, stoppered bottles :— *[Developing Solutions.]*

A.	B.
Stock Solution, 2 ounces.	Carbonate of Soda (Crystals), 2 ounces.
Water, 18 ounces.	Sulphite of Soda, 2 ounces.
	Bromide of Potassium, 20 grains.
	Water to 20 ounces.

Immediately before using, 6 drachms of A solution are added to the same quantity of B solution. A colourless mixture results.

Stains from this developer can be removed by the application of a weak solution of citric or hydrochloric acid; but as cleanliness of the hands and *[Removal of Stains.]*

Hydro-quinone: its advantages. fingers is a matter of great importance to the dental student, he is recommended to use hydroquinone. It has the advantages of not staining the fingers, can be used repeatedly, is suitable for plates and papers alike, and the negatives exhibit more detail, and are altogether softer than those obtained, under like conditions, with pyrogallic acid. A convenient formula is:—

A.	B.
Hydroquinone, 160 grains.	Sodium Hydrate, 100 grains.
Potassium Bromide, 30 grains.	Water, 20 ounces.
Sodium Sulphite, 2 ounces (Avoirdupois).	
Water to 20 ounces.	

For use, take equal quantities of each solution.

Development of Plates. The developer is to be poured evenly over the plate so that all its surface may be covered at once. The solution is kept in motion by a rocking movement of the dish, which should be held at some distance from the light. An occasional, rapid glance at the plate will suffice to tell how the development is proceeding; the criterion of complete development being afforded by the appearance of a faint black image seen *through* the glass, on the reverse side of the plate.

"Fixing." The negative must now be removed from the developer, washed quickly under water, and at once placed in a bath of hyposulphite of soda, $\frac{1}{4}$ lb., and water 20 ozs. After a few minutes fixation is complete, and the negative can be examined in full light.

Washing. Copious washing of the negative should next take place, and the plate be afterwards put into a rack to dry.

Printing.—The clearness of detail observed in prints made on Ilford Printing Out Paper, or Eastman's "Solio" renders these classes of papers suitable for photo-micrography. The student is recommended to use these papers, and to follow the instructions, as to manipulation, suggested by the manufacturers. Toning in a bath consisting of chloride of gold, 3 grains; sulphocyanide of ammonium, 30 grains; and cold water, 18 ounces, should be allowed to proceed until marked contrasts between the blacks and whites are noticed. *Toning Bath.*

Final Treatment.—A finished glossy appearance may be given to prints by adopting the following simple method:—A sheet of clear glass, free from scratches or other defects, should be thoroughly cleaned by brushing with soap and water. It is then dried, and French chalk powdered over it. This is removed by wiping with a dry clean rag, and the print, after having been soaked in clean water, is squeezed face downwards on to the glass, without excessive pressure, care being taken to remove all air-bubbles. If the print is then put into direct sunlight, it can be stripped off the glass, without sticking or tearing, at the end of two or three hours. Slip-in mounts are useful for holding the finished prints. *Finishing Prints.*

The Causes of Failure.

The chief causes that interfere with the production of satisfactory photo-micrographs, other than those arising from defective apparatus, may be here enumerated, and remedies suggested for the prevention of failure.

(1) The section may be too thick, or incorrectly stained, or improperly mounted. Only uniformly thin sections can be satisfactorily photographed—they must not be thick in some places and thin in others. *Sections.*

The more commonly used stains for sections to be photographed may be divided into two classes— *Correct Staining.*

good and indifferent. To the former belong aniline blue black, Bismark brown, and hæmatoxylene, especially when this is of a clear dark blue colour. Of the latter class, picro-carmine, eosine, and rubine are perhaps the best. The staining must not be too dense. In certain cases, when objects present only shades of a single colour, the interposition of a coloured screen (which can be purchased at opticians) between the illuminant and the section, produces better negatives than the employment of isochromatic plates alone. The tint of the screen should be the complement of the colour of the stain—that is, one which nearly reduces the colour of the image to a neutral grey. Thus an orange tinted screen is to be used when a blue stained preparation is to be photographed. Picro-carmine gives good results alone, but is improved by using a light green screen. The length of exposure will, under these circumstances, be necessarily prolonged.

The Use of Screens.

The mountant should be colourless or nearly so. Canada balsam sometimes acquires a yellow tinge after having been kept for a long period, but it is the best medium to use. The section must be perfectly flat. It is advisable always to use a strong clip to press down the cover glass uniformly, immediately after mounting.

Correct Mounting.

(2) There will be blurring of the image on the sensitive plate, if precautions are not taken to keep the apparatus firmly fixed, and free from vibrations. The cardboard screen should always be used.

(3) Plates may be under or over exposed, by which is meant that negatives may either be lacking in detail, or "flat," that is, present no degrees of contrast. It is useless to endeavour to improve an improperly exposed negative, either by intensification or any other method. Experience alone will enable

Under and Over Exposure.

the operator to judge the correct length of exposure: he must take into account the intensity of the illuminant, the size of the diaphragm, the power of the objective, and the staining of the section.

(4) The plates and developing solutions if old will not yield such good results as if they are new. Small quantities of both should be obtained at a time. *Developers.*

By careful attention to the foregoing details, the difficulties of making sharp, bright negatives should be removed.*

Method of ascertaining the amplification of an object.—The approximate camera magnification of an object may be learnt by means of very convenient rules suggested by Mr. G. P. Vereker in the *Photographic Quarterly*, Vol. III., No. 10. He writes:—"In using a microscope it must be looked upon as a double lens, or, if the objective alone is used, a single lens. Many different magnifications can be got out of one objective and eyepiece. The initial power of the lens is found by dividing 10 (the nearest average distance of distinct vision in inches) by the focus of the objective. Thus 10 divided by $\frac{1}{4}$ = 40, which is the initial power of $\frac{1}{4}$ in. objective. Multiply this by the power of the eyepiece, and the magnifying power of the combination results. Thus, if the eyepiece magnifies 5, the combination with the $\frac{1}{4}$ inch objective will equal 200 diameters. *Vereker's Rules.*

If the eyepiece and objective are used:—

As 10 is to the camera length, so is the microscopic amplification to that of the camera. Thus, if *Rule.*

---

* For a fuller account of the art, the reader is referred to Mr. Andrew Pringle's excellent work, "Practical Photo-micrography," 1894.

¼ objective and A ocular are used, and the camera extends 12 inches, then:—

As 10 : 12 :: 200 : 240; magnification = 240 diameters.

Rule.

If the objective alone is used, the length of the microscope tube is added. Thus, if ¼ inch objective is used, and the microscope tube is 10 inches in length, and the camera extends 12 inches:—

As 10 : 12 + 10 :: 40 : 88; magnification = 88 diameters.

The rules above indicated are sufficient for the purpose of enabling the student to approximately compute the magnifications produced by any objectives he may employ.

CONCLUSION.

It need only be added that in practical dental microscopy, as in other scientific pursuits, common sense, thoroughness, attention to detail, and perseverance, will lead the enquirer to the not-far-distant goal of success; and instead of becoming a mere *dilletante*, he will develope into an enthusiastic worker in the science and art of dental microscopy.

APPENDIX.

APPENDIX.

NOTE I.

Nasmyth's Membrane.—Paul's Method of Preparation. This, the latest method of procedure, is the best yet devised for bringing out the reticulated appearance of Nasmyth's membrane, and is to be recommended in addition to the methods previously described. (*See* p. 22.)

In a 2 per cent. solution of Bichromate of Ammonium are placed several fully-developed unworn teeth of man, monkey, or sheep. They remain in this hardening fluid for a month, the fluid itself being constantly changed. After washing, they are transferred to two or three changes of alcohol and then placed in a mixture of 5 per cent. nitric acid and weak spirit. When the enamel is sufficiently decalcified, the tooth is immersed in water, and the membrane teased from off its surface with needle points. The membrane should be finally stained with eosine and mounted in Farrant's medium. In this manner its structure is rendered apparent, and the use of silver nitrate for staining purposes dispensed with. (*Dental Record*, Vol. XIV., p. 562.)

NOTE II.

Hæmatoxylene Staining Solutions.—The following formulæ will be found to be useful to the advanced student :—

(i.) Delafield's Stain—
    Hæmatoxylene (crystals) ... 4 grammes.
    Absolute alcohol ... ... 25 c.c.
To be added to
    Ammonia alum (Sat. aq. sol.) ... 400 c.c.

Expose to light and air for several days, then filter and add

Glycerine (pure)	100 c.c.
Methylic alcohol	100 c.c.

A sufficient quantity of this mixture is to be added to distilled water to make a very dilute solution.

This is altogether the most powerful and precise of all the hæmatoxylene stains yet introduced.

(ii.) Ehrlich's Stain—

Hæmatoxylene (crystals)	2 grammes.
Absolute alcohol	100 c.c.

To be added to

Glycerine (pure)	100 c.c.
Ammonia alum	2 grammes.
Glacial acetic acid	10 c.c.
Distilled water	100 c.c.

The stain retains its properties for years if kept in well-stoppered bottles, and can be used for staining *en masse*.

(iii.) Kleinenberg's Stain—

Hæmatoxylene (crystals)	$2\frac{1}{2}$ grammes.
Rectified spirits of wine	240 c.c.

To be added to the two following solutions:—

Calcium chloride (crystals)	20 grammes.
Distilled water	10 c.c.

And

Alum	3 grammes.
Distilled water	16 c.c.

The above is Squire's modification of the original formulæ. It is highly recommended for the certainty of its results.

Carmine Staining Solutions:

(i.) Beale's Stain—

Carmine...	10 grains.
Strong solution of ammonia	30 minims.

To be added, after boiling and evaporation, to

Glycerine (pure)	2 ounces.
Alcohol	$\frac{1}{2}$ ounce.
Distilled water	2 ounces.

A useful general stain.

(ii.) Grenacher's Stain—
    Carmine ... ...   3 grammes.
    Borax ... ...   4 grammes.
    Distilled water ... ...   100 c.c.
To be added, after gentle heating, to
    Alcohol (70%)... ... ...   100 c.c.

The student is cautioned against the use of Grenacher's *alum* carmine stain, as it has a dissolving action on all calcareous structures, and therefore soon destroys the hard parts of his dental sections. By the employment of the above, this inconvenience is avoided.

(iii.) Orth's Stain—
    Carmine ... ... $2\frac{1}{2}$ grammes.
To be added to 100 c.c. of
    Carbonate of Lithium ... ...   7 grammes.
    Distilled water ... ...   700 c.c.

This is both a nuclear and plasmatic stain. But if acidulated alcohol is used after staining, in the manner described on page 68, the colouring of the cell substance is removed, but that of the nucleus is still retained.

NOTE III.

Actinic and visual foci.—Actinic is the name given to that property of light which chemically affects the film of a sensitive photographic plate. The term "visual focus" means the sharpness and clearness of the image which is thrown on the camera screen, when seen by the observer's eye. But it sometimes happens that, although the image may appear sharply defined to the eye, it is not photographically in focus: the two foci are then said to be non-coincident. This occurs in "uncorrected" lenses. Should it be found that the foci do not coincide, the uncorrected objective must be slightly moved from or advanced towards the object, the motion which is necessary and the extent of it, being found by actual experiment and carefully recorded. (*See* p. 97.)

INDEX.

	PAGE
Absorbent Organ, To Make Sections of	35
Acids, Use of	19
Actinic Focus	97, 110
Ady's Method of Mounting Sections	79
Air Bubbles, Removal of	78
Avoidance of...	77
Alcohol	29
Alveolar Bone, To Make Sections of	49
Amplification of Objects in Photomicrography	105
Andrew's Method of Preparing Hard Sections	18
Aqueous Mountants	82
Arkansas Stones for polishing	15, 18
Artificial Injection of Blood-vessels	86
Balsam, Canada, for Mounting	77
In Weil's Process	42
Spokes on	80
For Calcified and Uncalcified Tissues	79, 80
Beale's Injection Mass	87
Tint Reflector	90
Stain	109
Bennett on Laminæ in Dentine	24
Black's Acid Solution	20
Pigmentation Stain...	71
Blood Supply of Teeth	35
Bödecker's Method of Decalcification	21
Bumpus on Clearing Celloidin Imbedded Sections	60
Calcified Tissues, Mounting	79, 80
Camera for Photomicrography	95

INDEX.

	PAGE
Campion's Method of Hardening Soft Tissues	32
Carmine Stain	68, 109, 110
Cathcart's Microtome	54
Caush's Method of Preparing Sections of Hard and Soft Tissues in situ	48
Celloidin, Imbedding in	58
Cements for Ringing Slides	84
Cementum, To make Sections of	23, 25
Chart, Micrometer	91
Charters White's Method of Preparing Hard Tissues	15
Mounting in Balsam	79
Stain	74
Chloroform	42
Choquet on Decalcifying Solutions	45
Chromic Acid, Process for Hard and Soft Tissues combined	39
As a Decalcifying Agent	19
As a Stain	72
Clearing Sections	75
Condenser, Bull's eye	8
Substage	7
Contrast Stains	72
To Hæmatoxylene	67
To Carmine	69
Cover Glasses	10
How to Apply	77
Cutting Serial Sections	60

Decalcified Tissues, Method of Mounting	77, 80
Decalcification of Hard Tissues	18
Dehydration of Sections	66
Special	75
Delafield's Hæmatoxylene Stain	108
Dental Follicle, To Obtain Specimens of	35
Dental Gum, To Make Sections of	35
Dental Pulp, To Make Sections of	36
Dentine, To Make Sections of	23

INDEX. 113

	PAGE
Developing Sensitive Plates	102
Solutions	101
Developmental Tissues, Preparation of	30
Diagrams, Use of	94
Drawing Microscopical Specimens	92
Dunkerley's Method of Cutting Hard Sections ...	17
Ebner's Decalcifying Fluid	21
Enamel, Decalcification of	22
Grinding Hard Sections of	16
Eosine	67, 69
Embryonic Tissues	31
Ehrlich's Hæmatoxylene Stain	109
Erlicki's Solution for Hardening Tissues	29
Ether	55
Ether-freezing Microtome, Use of	54
Examination of Sections	11
Exercise, Preliminary	12
Exposure of Sensitive Plates in Photomicrography ...	100
To Obtain Approximate Duration of	100
Failure, Causes of, in Photomicrography	103
Farrant's Mounting Medium	82
Finishing Slides	84
Photographic Prints	103
Fish's Teeth, To Make Sections of	25
Fixing Soft Tissues	27
Flemming's Method of Mounting	80
Flotation, Mounting by	81
Follicle, Dental, Preparation of	35
Formic Acid	21, 70
Fuchsine	76
General Stains	65
Glycerine Methods, Bennett's	24
Glycerine Jelly	82
Gold Chloride for Staining Tissues	70

	PAGE
Golgi's Method of Staining	73
Grenacher's Carmine	68, 110
Grinding Specimens of Hard Tissues	15
Gubernaculum, Preparation of	35
Gum Mucilage for Soft Tissues	31
For Imbedding	53
In Author's Process...	47
Hæmatoxylene	67
Delafield's	108
Ehrlich's	109
Kleinenberg's	109
Weigert's	74
Hard Dental Tissues, Table of	25
Hardening Soft Tissues	27
Hart's Decalcifying Method	21
Hindostan Stones for Grinding Down Sections ...	18
Histological Classification of Tissues	30
Hopewell Smith's Process	44
Summary of	50
Hydrochloric Acid	20
Hydroquinone	102
Imbedding, Object of	52
In Celloidin	58
In Gum	53
In Paraffin	61
Interstitial	53
Immersion, Staining by	65
Injection of Blood Vessels	86
Mass	87
Instruments for Drawing Objects	92
Mansbridge's List of	8
Interglobular Spaces, Preparation of	25
Staining of	71

INDEX. 115

	PAGE
Jaws of Animals, Preparation of, fœtal...	31
At Birth	32
Fully Developed	25
Kleinenberg's Decalcifying Solution	21
Hæmatoxylene Stain	109
Laminæ in Dentine	24
Lenses for Photomicrography	96
Lepkowski's Method of Decalcification	21
Magnification of Sections	11
Of Photomicrographs	105
Mansbridge's List of Instruments	8
Method of Mounting in Balsam	79
Marchi's Stain	73
Marson's Method of Hardening Soft Tissues	34
Matrix in Weil's Process	44
Measurement of Objects	89
Mercury Perchloride	32, 41
Methylated Spirit	30
Methylene Blue	69
Micrometer, Stage	89
Ocular	91
Chart	91
Microscope, Makers of	4
Method of Using	10
Parts of	6
Microtomes, Cathcart's	54
Rocking	62
Roy's	57
Swift's	56
Mirrors of Microscope	7
Mounting, Correct, for Photomicrography	104

INDEX.

	PAGE
Mounting Sections	75
Serial Sections	82
Müller's Fluid	28
Mummery, Howard, on Imbedding in Paraffin	61
On Iron Staining	72
On Weil's Process	43
Nasmyth's Membrane, Preparation of	22
Paul's Method of Preparation of	108
Natural Injection of Capillaries	86
Nerves of Pulp, Preparation of	36
Method of Staining	72
Neumann, Sheaths of, Preparation of	23
Objectives	3, 7, 96
Ocular Micrometer	91
Odontoblasts	37
Orth's Carmine	110
Osmic Acid, for Fixing Tissues	27
As a Stain	71
Over-exposed Negatives	104
Owen's Lines, To Make Sections to show	25
Paper Cell for Imbedding in Celloidin	59
Paraffin, Imbedding in	61
Paul's Method of Preparing Sections of Nasmyth's Membrane	108
Peridental Membrane, To Make Sections of	32, 51
Photomicrographic Apparatus	95
Pigmentation Stain, Osmic Acid as	71
Plates, Sensitive	98
Preparation of Hard Tissues	14
Preparation of Soft Tissues	26
Preparation of Hard and Soft Tissues Combined	39

INDEX. 117

	PAGE
Pulp, Dental, To Make Sections of	36, 51
Pyrogallic Acid	101
Rack for Wolrab's Bottles	9
Resin and Wax	16
Retention of Soft Parts in situ	39
Retzius, Striæ of, Preparation of Sections of	25
Ringing Slides	84
Robertson's Aitchison, Method of Making Sections of Odontoblasts	37
Rocking Microtome	62
Room for Photomicrography	95
Rothmann's Methods of Preparing Sections of Soft Tissues	34
Roy's Microtome	57
Method of Using	58
Rubbing Down Sections between Glass Plates	16
Rubine	69
Rules for Ascertaining Amplification of Objects in Photomicrography	105
Salt Solution, Normal	22, 45, 82
Scale, Micrometric	91
Schreger's Lines, To Obtain Sections Shewing	25
Screen for use with Microscope	8
For Photomicrography	104
Sections Hard, Soft, and Hard and Soft Combined, Preparation of	14, 26, 39
Serial Section Cutting	60
Shrinkage, To Prevent	26
Silver Nitrate, For Staining Tissues	72
Soluble Glass	16, 82
Special Stains	73
Specific Stains	69

	PAGE
Spokes, On Finishing Sections	44
On Mounting Sections	80
Stage, Micrometer	89
Staining, Correct, for Photomicrography	103
Staining Teased-out Specimens...	66
Staining Tissues, Advantages of	64
General Methods	65
By Immersion	65
By Transfusion	66
Substage, Microscope	7
Sudduth's Method of Hardening Tissues	28
Sulphindigotate of Soda...	69
Summary of Weil's Process	49
Summary of Author's Process	50
Swift's Microtome	56
Table of Hard Tissues, Suitable for Decalcification or Grinding Down	25
Table of Soft Tissues	38
Table of Hard and Soft Tissues Combined	51
Table of Tissues Suitable for Imbedding in Gum, Celloidin or Paraffin	63
Table of Tissues, Suitable for Various Stains	76
Tannin and Iron Stain	72
Teasing-out Specimens	39
Teased-out Specimens, Staining	66
Teeth of Horse and Fish, Preparation of ...	18, 25
Thyme, Oil of	60
Tint Reflector, Beale's	90
Toning Bath for Photographic Prints...	103
Transference, Mounting by	77
Transfusion, Staining by	66
Turntable	84
Under-exposed Negatives	104
Underwood's Method of Gold Staining ...	70
Unmounting Sections	83

	PAGE
Vascular Injections	86
Vereker on Amplification of Objects in Photo-micrography	105
Visual Focus	110

Washita Stone	43
Water of Ayr Stone for Polishing Sections	17
Weigert's Stain	74
Weil's Hardening Fluid	28
Process	41
Summary of	49
Whittle's Lathe	18
Wolrab's Bottles	20
Wulff's Bottles	87

Xylol	42, 78

www.ingramcontent.com/pod-product-compliance
Lightning Source LLC
Chambersburg PA
CBHW030352170426
43202CB00010B/1353